Aquinas Thomas, William Humphrey

Memoranda of Angelical Doctrine

A Digest of the Doctrine of S. Thomas on the Sacraments

Aquinas Thomas, William Humphrey

Memoranda of Angelical Doctrine
A Digest of the Doctrine of S. Thomas on the Sacraments

ISBN/EAN: 9783337330958

Printed in Europe, USA, Canada, Australia, Japan

Cover: Foto ©Lupo / pixelio.de

More available books at **www.hansebooks.com**

PREFACE.

THE following pages contain, as their title-page indicates, a digest of, not a commentary on, the Doctrine of S. Thomas on the Sacraments; and a digest the writer has endeavoured to give *ad mentem* of his great author, but without note or comment to shew the agreement of his teaching with, or its divergence from, other schools of theological thought, ancient, mediæval, or modern, Greek, Latin, or English.

He will never cease to grieve if his work deters or prevents any one student of Theology from the study, in the original, of the wonderful treatise from which it is derived.

The Memoranda will, he believes, be found useful by two classes of persons. By those who have not yet entered on the study of Sacramental Theology, as a chart to give them some idea of that beautiful land as yet unknown to them: to those also who have made some progress in it, as an itinerary of their journey, and as reminiscences of the way.

He has appended to it the axioms of Hunnæus, while a Scheme of the same learned writer will serve by way of Index.

Such as it is, he commends his work to God, and dedicates it
Sancto, Sanctæ, Sanctis,
to all who, being many, are One in the Sacramental Jesus.

S. Mary the Virgin,
The Cove, near Aberdeen, N.B.,
Lent, 1867.

CONTENTS.

I.	Sacraments in General,	1
II.	Baptism,	10
III.	Confirmation,	21
IV.	The Eucharist,	26
V.	Penance,	59
VI.	Extreme Unction,	95
VII.	Orders,	105
VIII.	Matrimony,	120
IX.	The Axioms of Hunnæus,	155

The Sacraments of the Church.

1. SACRAMENTS IN GENERAL.

I. ALL things which have an order to any one thing may be denominated therefrom; and so any thing may be called a Sacrament which, 1, has in it a hidden sanctity: and according to this a Sacrament is the same as a secret sacredness; or, 2, as having an order to sanctify whether as cause, or sign, or otherwise. The sanctity from which the word Sacrament is derived is a cause—but formal or final, and not efficient—however theologians generally speak of Sacraments as they are signs, and so place them in the genus of signs. In this way S. Augustine writes, 10 de Civit. Dei, A visible sacrifice is the sacrament, that is, the sacred sign of an invisible sacrifice. And a sign he in another place defines to be that which, besides the appearance which it presents to the senses, causes something else to come into the mind. But when we use the word Sacrament, we do not thereby mean every sign of a sacred reality, but only such signs as signify realities pertaining to men and their sanctification. And these signs are given to men because it is a condition of their present existence to arrive at the unknown by means of the known. The Sacraments of the old law were so called because they signified the sanctity of Christ, whereby we are sanctified.

II. A Sacrament is a sign *rememorative* of that which is past, viz., the Passion of Christ, which is *the cause* of our sanctification; *demonstrative* of that which is wrought in us thereby, viz., Divine Grace and Virtue, which is *the form* of our sanctification; and prognostick or *prenuntiative* of the future glory, viz., Life eternal, which is the last end, and *final cause* of our sanctification.

III. The Divine Wisdom which sweetly disposeth all things, provides for every thing according to its mode, as It gives to each according to its several ability. Now it is connatural to man to arrive at a knowledge of the intelligible through the sensible, that is, at a knowledge of those things which form the subject matter of his intellect, by means of those things which present themselves to his senses. And so he arrives at those sacred realities, those spiritual and intelligible goods whereby he is sanctified, by means of certain *outward sensible things* called signs; for that whereby one arrives at the knowledge of something else is its sign.

IV. It does not appertain to one to determine that which is in the power of another, but that only which is in his own power. And so, since man's sanctification is not in his own but in God's power, it belongs to God and not to man to determine the means whereby it shall be accomplished. To determine the sign belongs to the signifier, whether that sign be sensible sacraments or verbal similitudes, as in the Scriptures. Men must, therefore, use those signs which have been *divinely determined*, in order to their sanctification; and the way of salvation is not hereby straitened, because the necessary matter is either universally possessed or may easily be procured.

V. It was most fitting that in the Sacraments, *words* should be united to *sensible things*, 1, by reason of the sanctifying cause, which is the Incarnate Word, that is, the Word of God united to sensible flesh; 2, by reason of man, who is sanctified. He is composed of body and soul. By the sensible matter the sacramental medicine is conveyed to his body, by the words it is exhibited to his soul. 3, By reason of the sacramental signification. By words we express with our lips what we conceive in our minds. The word, says S. Augustine, comes to the element, and the Sacrament is made.

There was no form of words required before the Incarnation of the Word in the sacraments of the Old Law.

The words have themselves by way of *form* as the sensible things by way of *matter;* the matter is determinate, à *fortiori* is the form which is its end and term.

VI. The words wherein the form of the sacraments consists may not be added to or taken from in such wise as to corrupt their true sense.

VII. Sacraments are necessary in order to man's salvation for three reasons. 1. From the condition of human nature ; of which it is a property to arrive at the spiritual and intelligible, through the corporal and sensible. 2. From the estate of man ; who by sinning, subjected his affections to corporal things. 3. To preserve him from the superstitious use of these, to which he would be prone, if altogether deprived of their religious use.

And so by means of Sacraments man is, 1, instructed, 2, humbled, and, 3, preserved from sin. As S. Augustine says: Under no name of religion, be it true or false, can men be united, unless they be bound together by some fellowship of visible signs or sacraments.

VIII. In the *estate of innocence* man did not need sacraments, 1, either as a remedy for sin; for they that are whole have no need of a physician, and spiritual medicines are necessary only for sin-sick souls ; 2, or in order to the perfection of his soul. For in unfallen man his various component parts preserved their due order ; the higher governed the lower, and was in no way dependent thereupon. For as the mind was subject to God, so to the mind were subject the inferior powers of the soul, and to the soul was subject the body : and it would have been inconsistent with this order that the soul should derive perfection from any corporal thing, such as a sacrament.

True, in the estate of innocence man needed *grace*, but it does not follow that he needed to receive it sacramentally : it was fitting, on the contrary, that he should receive it spiritually and invisibly. For although the nature of man after sin is the same as before, it is not in the same state.

Matrimony was instituted in the estate of innocence, 1, for a function of nature. 2. After sin, for a remedy of lust. 3. Under grace, and not till then, as a sacrament, signifying the union of the Bridegroom and the Bride, Christ and the Catholick Church.

IX. Since after sin no man can be sanctified save by Christ, it was necessary that during the period after sin, but before His Advent, there should exist certain sacraments as signs and protestations of men's faith in Him.

X. As the old fathers were saved by faith in the coming Christ, so are we saved by faith in Him who has been born and suffered. And so, as the sacraments of the Old Law were *signs of the future*, the sacraments of the New Law are *signs of the past*. As S. Augustine says: the sacraments of the Old Law were taken away because they were fulfilled, and others have been instituted, exceeding them in power, excelling them in usefulness, easier in performance, and fewer in number.

XI. The sacraments of the Old Law *neither contained nor caused grace;* and so the Apostle calls them weak and beggarly elements, and those who used them he speaks of as in bondage under the elements of the world, than which these sacraments were nothing more.

XII. The estate of the New Law stands midway between the estate of the Old Law and the estate of Glory, when the Truth will be manifested nakedly, perfectly, and openly. Now we see through a glass, and as in an enigma; and so now we need sensible signs whereby to arrive at things spiritual: then there will be no sacraments when we stand face to face, when we see as we are seen, and know even as we are ourselves known.

XIII. Although God alone is the effective and principal cause of grace, yet the sacraments of the New Law cause grace by way of instrument. When an instrumental cause is manifest it may be called also the sign of a hidden effect. And so the Sacraments are *at once causes and signs,* hence the common theological expression—that *they effect what they figure.*

XIV. Grace perfects the essence of the soul by causing it to be, as S. Peter says, a partaker of the Divine nature; and as from the essence of the soul proceed its powers, so from grace proceed certain perfections of those powers in order to their several acts. These are called virtues and gifts.

XV. Sacramental grace adds, over and above the grace of virtues and gifts, a Divine *aid in order to attain the end* of the sacrament; as virtues and gifts add, over and above grace, a determinate perfection, in order to the acts of their several and special powers. By virtues and gifts sins and vices are sufficiently excluded as to the present and future, inasmuch, viz., as a man is hindered by virtues and gifts from sinning; but as to past sins, which pass away in act, but remain in liability to punishment, a remedy is specially applied to man by the sacraments.

XVI. The Sacraments of the New Law contain grace as the instrumental cause is said to contain the effect.

XVII. There is in the sacraments a certain instrumental power to produce grace, which is an effect of the sacrament proportioned to its instrumental character. It is not permanent, but transient, as an instrument does not operate save as moved by the principal agent.

XVIII. The Sacraments are instrumental causes of grace. But instruments are of two sorts, separate as a staff, conjunct as a hand. By the conjunct instrument the separate instrument is moved as is the staff by the hand. Now the *principal efficient cause* of grace is God Himself. To Him is related the Humanity of Christ as a *conjunct instrument*, and a sacrament as a *separate instrument*. And so the saving power is derived from the Divinity of Christ to the sacraments by means of His Humanity.

Christ by His Passion wrought both our freedom from sin and our sanctification, not only sufficiently and meritoriously, but also satisfactorily. Of the virtue of His Passion are we made partakers by reception of the sacraments; and so it is true to say that they have all their efficacy from the Passion of Christ. In token whereof there flowed from the Side of Christ, as He slept on the Cross, water and blood, whereof the one pertains to Baptism and the other to the Eucharist, which are the (*potissima*) principal Sacraments.

XIX. Since the efficient cause can never be posterior to its effect, the sacraments of the Old Law preceding the Passion of Christ, which is the cause of our justification, had no power *in themselves* of conferring justifying grace, although *by faith of the Passion* of Christ the old fathers were justified as are we; the sacraments of the Old Law being protestations of that faith, inasmuch as they signified the Passion of Christ and its effects.

Had they contained and conferred grace then the Passion would not have been necessary, as S. Paul taught the Galatians: "If righteousness come by the law, then Christ is dead in vain."

XX. *Character* is a note or sign impressed or affixed to anything whereby it may be distinguished from others. Of this nature were the red crosses on the garments of the Spanish soldiers, and the white crosses of the French—the signs branded with a red-hot iron on traitors and slaves—and of the same nature is *sacramental character*. It is a sign or spiritual seal impressed on our souls by God, whereby we are distinguished from others who lack this spiritual note, and wherewith we are sealed as the soldiers of God and Christ, and destined to the spiritual warfare, the worship of God, and the practice of the Christian religion. Grieve not, says S. Paul to the Ephesians, the Holy Spirit of God whereby we are *sealed* unto the day of redemption. And again: In Whom also, after that ye believed, ye were *sealed* with that Holy Spirit of Promise. And to the Corinthians he writes: He who hath anointed us is God, who hath also *sealed* us, and given the earnest of the Spirit in our hearts.

XXI. The Divine worship consists either in the reception of Divine things oneself or in the tradition of them to others. In either case is required power—for tradition, an *active power;* for reception, a *passive power*. This passive power is conferred in Baptism, which fits, disposes, and gives one a right to receive the other sacraments. The active power is conferred in Holy Orders in order to the instrumental tradition of Divine things to others.

XXII. The whole rite of the Christian religion is derived from the Priesthood of Christ; and so the *sacramental character* is specially the *character* of Christ, which is derived to the faithful inasmuch as they share His Priesthood, who is the Brightness of the Father's Glory, and the Express Image, or *character*, of His Person.

XXIII. *Character is indelible*—1, being a participation of the Priesthood of Christ, which is eternal; and, 2, the intellect, which is that part of the rational soul which is its subject, being perpetual and incorruptible.

XXIV. Character remains after this life; in the just to their glory: in the wicked to their shame.

XXV. Since by Baptism, Confirmation, and Orders alone a man is ordained either to the reception or the tradition of those things which pertain to the Divine Worship, there are only these three sacraments of the New Law which impress *character*, and which may not therefore be iterated. By penance a man is simply restored to his former state; while in the Blessed Eucharist the Divine Worship principally consists, inasmuch as it is the Sacrifice of the Church, and the end and consummation of all the Sacraments; which contains in it Christ Himself, in whom there is not *character*, but the whole plenitude of priesthood.

The power of the priesthood is related to *character* as is that which is perfect and complete to that which is its participation.

XXVI. Although God alone works as the principal agent in order to the interior effect of the sacraments, yet man may work ministerially for the same end.

The virtue of the sacraments being from God alone as the principal agent, He alone is the Institutor of them. Those actions in the sacraments which are of human institution are *not of necessity* to the sacrament, but for the sake of solemnity, and in order to excite devotion and reverence in those who receive them. But all those things which are of necessity to the sacraments were instituted by the God-man. And although they be not all delivered in the Scriptures, yet the Church has received them from the familiar tradition of the Apostles. To such the Apostle refers when he says to the Corinthians: The rest will I set in order when I come. As the Apostles and their successors the Vicars of God upon earth, may not establish another Church, or deliver another Faith, so they may not institute other sacraments.

XXVII. Christ operates the interior effect of the sacraments, both as He is God and as He is man, but differently in either case. As He is God He operates by authority, and as principal agent; as He is man, meritoriously and efficiently, but instrumentally.

His power of excellence and principal ministry consists in four things—1, In that the merit and virtue of the Passion operates in the sacraments; 2, in that in His Name the sacraments are sanctified; 3, in that He who gave the sacraments their virtue could institute them; and, 4, He could Himself alone, without the sacraments, have justified man.

His power as God He can no more communicate to a creature than He can the Divine Essence; but His powers as man He can and does communicate to His ministers.

XXVIII. The ministers of the Church, being instruments, can confer the sacraments, whether they be good or evil, the Lord of the Sacraments being the good God. The sin of evil ministers ministering the sacraments is mortal, as involving irreverence. As long as a minister is tolerated by the Church in the ministry, he who receives from him a sacrament does not communicate in his sin, but communicates with the Church, which sets him forth as her minister. But if he be not tolerated, that is to say, when he is degraded or excommunicated, or suspended, he sins who receives from him a sacrament, because he communicates with and is made partaker of his sin.

XXIX. Since men alone are *conformed to Christ*, it pertains to men alone, and *not to angels*, to minister the sacraments; such ministry being a participation of the priesthood of Christ, which priesthood He exercises in as much as *He is man*.

But as God has not bound down His power to the sacraments, but can without them produce their effects, so, in like manner, He has not bound down His power to the ministers of the Church in such wise that He may not also impart it to angels.

XXX. Since those things which are done in the sacraments may be done in divers ways, and for various reasons, the intention of the minister or of the Church is necessary in their administration, which *intention is expressed* by the words used. And this suffices to the perfection of the sacrament, unless a contrary intention be outwardly expressed. As wicked ministers may confer sacraments, so may unbelieving ministers, provided they intend to do what the Church does, even although they believe that to be nothing; and, 2, that they omit none of those things which are of necessity to the sacrament.

XXXI. As the power of ministering the sacraments pertains to spiritual *character*, which is indelible, so a suspended, excommunicated, or even degraded priest does not lose *the power* of conferring the sacraments, but the license of using the power. He confers *the sacrament*, but not *the reality* of the sacrament; and he who receives at his hands sins mortally, unless he can plead invincible ignorance.

XXXII. The spiritual life has a certain conformity to the bodily life, both as respects man as an individual, and as a member of a society. 1. As an individual; in place of *generation* in the natural life, there is in the spiritual life Baptism, the Sacrament of *Regeneration*; in place of *increase of natural strength*, the Holy Ghost is given in Confirmation for the *increase of spiritual strength;* in place of *nourishment*, there is the *Eucharist*; and in place of *healing*, *Penitence*. Extreme unction removes the remains of sin, which by reason of negligence or ignorance have not been sufficiently destroyed by penitence. 2. As a member of a society, the power of *governing* and of exercising public acts is conferred by the Sacrament of *Order;* while in order to the *propagation* of individuals, both for the natural and the spiritual life, there is the Sacrament of *Matrimony.*

Baptism is ordained against the lack of spiritual life.
Confirmation, against feebleness of soul.
The Eucharist, against the soul's liability to sin.
Penitence, against actual and post-baptismal sin.
Extreme Unction, against the remains of sin in the penitent.
Order, against the breaking up of the multitude.
Matrimony, against concupiscence and loss of numbers.

Or again ;

Baptism corresponds to Faith, and is ordained against original sin.
Extreme Unction answers to Hope, and is ordained against venial sin.
The Eucharist corresponds to Charity, and is ordained against the punishment of wickedness.
Order corresponds to Prudence, and is ordained against ignorance.
Penitence corresponds to Justice, and is ordained against mortal sin.
Matrimony corresponds to Temperance, and is ordained against concupiscence.
Confirmation corresponds to Fortitude, and is ordained against infirmity.

XXXIII. The Eucharist is the chief among all the sacraments, 1, because It contains not the grace of Christ only, but Christ Himself. 2. Because all the other sacraments are ordained to It as to an end, as Order for Its consecration, Baptism for Its reception, Confirmation to perfect men so that they may not fear to approach, Penitence and Extreme Unction to prepare them to receive worthily, and Matrimony as signifying the union which It effects between Christ and His Church.

XXXIV. There are three sacraments necessary to salvation. Baptism, simply and absolutely ; Penitence, for those who have fallen into mortal sin after Baptism ; Order, in order to the existence and government of the Church. The others are necessary in so far, as by means of them the effect of salvation is most fittingly attained.

2. THE SACRAMENT OF BAPTISM.

XXXV. IN the Sacrament of Baptism there are three things to be considered: 1, that which is sacrament only; 2, that which is reality as well; 3, that which is reality (*res*) only. 1, that which is *sacrament only*, is the outward and visible sign of the inward effect, viz., water and its use, which is ablution; 2, that which is *sacrament and reality* as well, is the baptismal character which is the reality signified by the outward ablution, and is the sacramental sign of the inward justification, which justification is, 3, the *reality only*, to wit, that which is signified, and does not itself signify.

XXXVI. That which in Baptism is sacrament only passes away; 2, that which is reality as well, viz., character, remains indelibly; 3, that which is reality only, viz., justification, remains, but may be lost.

XXXVII. A sacrament may be said to be instituted when it receives the power of producing its effect, and so Baptism as it is a sacrament was instituted in the Baptism of Christ. But the necessity of using it was not enjoined on men till after His Passion and Resurrection. 1. Because then were terminated the figural Sacraments of the Old Law to which Baptism and the Sacraments of the New Law succeeded. 2. Because by Baptism a man is configurated and conformed to Christ's Passion and Resurrection, inasmuch as he dies unto sin and begins a new life unto righteousness.

XXXVIII. Of divine institution water is the proper matter of Baptism. And this fitly, 1, By reason of baptism being a regeneration to spiritual life; water being a principal agent in the generation of natural life, 2, By reason of the effects of baptism to which the properties of water correspond, i., by its humidity it washes, and so is fitted to signify and cause the washing away of sin; ii., by its frigidity it tempers the superfluity of heat; and baptism moderates the fires of concupiscence, iii., by its transparency it is susceptive of light, and baptism is the sacrament of Faith and Illumination. 3, By reason of its representing the mysteries of Christ whereby we are justified. The old man descends, is buried in, and rises again renewed from the water as from a sepulchre. 4, By reason of its commonness and abundance it is the fitting matter for the sacrament of necessity. It may be had with ease and everywhere.

XXXIX. Christ, by the touch of His most pure Flesh, conferred on water its regenerative and purgative power.

XL. Exorcism and Benediction are not of necessity to the sacrament of baptism, but are added for the sake of solemnity, to excite the devotion of the faithful, and to hinder the subtle malice of demons, who strive to prevent the baptism having effect.

XLI. Baptism may be made in any water, however mixed, altered, or changed, whether by nature or by art, so long as the species of water is not destroyed. But when the species of water is destroyed, as for instance, when it is so mixed with clay as to be more clay than water, or so mixed with wine as to be more wine than water, it may not be made in that.

XLII. The common form of baptism is fitting, inasmuch as it expresses both the principal and the instrumental cause. It expresses the instrumental cause, the minister, by the words, I baptize thee; and the principal cause, the Holy Trinity, by the words, In the name of the Father, and of the Son, and of the Holy Ghost. The Greeks do not attribute the act of baptism to the minister in order to discountenance the old error, that baptism owed its efficacy to its ministers, whence men said, I am of Paul and I of Cephas; and so they say, May the servant of Christ be baptized in the Name, &c. The Passion of Christ is the principal cause of baptism in respect of its minister, but the instrumental cause in respect of the Holy Trinity, and so in the form of words the Holy Trinity is commemorated rather than the Passion of Christ. Although the Three Persons have three personal names, yet having One Essence, they have one Essential Name. But the Divine Virtue which operates in Baptism belongs to the Divine Essence, and so we do not say In the Names, but In the Name. Again; water from its commonness has been appointed as the matter, and these personal names, the Father, the Son, and the Holy Ghost, have from their commonness been included in the form of baptism. Neither is there baptism in any other.

XLIII. Since Christ instituted the Sacrament of Baptism to be given with Invocation of the Trinity, it follows that the integrity of this sacrament is destroyed, if any thing be wanting which pertains to the full invocation of the Trinity. It will not suffice to baptize in the Name of Christ, nor will it suffice that by the Name of one person is understood the name of another, as in the Name of the Father is included the Name of the Son: nor that he who baptizes in the name of one has a right faith regarding the other two. In order to the perfection of this sacrament there is required a sensible form as well as sensible matter; and so in the Baptism of Christ, which was the origin of the sanctification of ours, the Trinity were present by sensible signs—the Father by His Voice, the Son in His Human Nature, and the Holy Spirit in the form of a Dove.

XLIV. Immersion is the more common and the safer use, but it is not of necessity to baptism, which may be made either by aspersion or by effusion, in case of necessity, by reason either of scarcity of water, or weakness, whether of the minister or the catechumen. Moreover, in Immersion is more expressly represented the figure of the Burial of Christ. When the whole body is not immersed, the head ought to be, as its principal part, and the residence of the senses. Ablution is essential: the mode of ablution is accidental.

XIV. Immersion, or aspersion, or effusion, so far as regards necessity and validity, may be single or trine. Both uses have at various times, and for divers reasons, mainly to discountenance and counteract then prevailing heresies, been ordered by the Church. And both significantly. The one represents the oneness of the Death of Christ, and the oneness of Deity; the trine represents the Trinity of Divine Persons, and the Three Days' Burial.

XLVI. Baptism may not be iterated. 1. Because it is a spiritual regeneration; and as carnal generation cannot be repeated, so neither can spiritual.

2. Because we are baptized unto the death of Christ, who died once. 3. Because it imprints indelible character, and sacraments which do so cannot be iterated. 4. Because it is mainly ordained against original sin, which cannot be iterated. In case of doubt as to whether a person has been baptized or not, he may be conditionally baptized with this form of words:—If thou art baptized, I baptize thee not, but if thou art not yet baptized, I baptize thee, &c.

XLVII. A man may attain the effect of baptism with water, that is, the being conformed to Christ, by suffering for Christ, and also by the interior working of the Holy Ghost, moving him to repentance and faith and love, and so there are three baptisms. 1. The baptism of water. 2. The baptism of the Spirit, or of repentance, and 3. The baptism of blood. The Passion of Christ operates in the Baptism of Water by a figural representation, in the Baptism of the Spirit by an affection, but in the Baptism of Blood by imitation. Again the power of the Holy Ghost operates in baptism by a latent virtue, in the baptism of repentance by a moving of the heart, but in the baptism of blood by the greatest fervour of love and affection ; and so of the three, the baptism of blood is the principal as to its effect. It includes the baptism of the Spirit, but not *e converso*.

XLVIII. From the very name of Deacon, *i.e.*, Minister, it is clear that it does not belong to him of his own office to confer the Sacrament of Baptism, but in the conferring of this and other sacraments, to assist and minister to his superiors. It properly belongs to the office of a Priest, although of course it belongs also to a Bishop, to baptize; the power of the superior including also that of the inferior. Since to a Priest it belongs as his proper office to consecrate the Eucharist, which is the sacrament of ecclesiastical unity, to a Priest it belongs also to minister the Sacrament of Baptism, whereby one is made a partaker of this unity, and acquires a right to receive the Eucharist. It has, however, been ordained, by the mercy of Him who wills all men to be saved, that in like manner as the matter of this Sacrament, which of all the Sacraments is of the greatest necessity, is to be had easily and everywhere, so any man, even a layman, may, in case of necessity, be the minister of this Sacrament, lest for want of the regeneration to spiritual life, and the full remission of the guilt and punishment of sin therein conveyed, any one should suffer loss. A layman, who in case of necessity is called on to baptize, will confine himself to the mere necessities, and in no case add the solemnities of baptism, such as exorcism; benediction of the water and the like. If he baptizes without necessity he sins; his act is nevertheless valid, and may not be iterated.

XLIX. It is Christ who is the principal minister, and really baptizes; but in Him there is neither male nor female, and so a woman may baptize as the minister of Christ. But as the man is the head of the woman, even as Christ is the head of the man, so a woman may not baptize in presence of a man, in like manner as a layman may not baptize in presence of a Clerk, nor a Clerk in presence of a Priest; but a Priest may baptize in presence of a Bishop, because to his office of a Priest the administration of baptism properly belongs. With regard to the solemnities of baptism, and to the sinfulness, although validity, of unnecessary baptism, the same remarks apply in the case of a woman as in the case of a layman. Even a person who is himself unbaptized, a Jew or a Pagan, may confer the Sacrament of Baptism, so that he use the due matter and form.

L. As infants, new born by carnal generation, are delivered to nurses and pedagogues to be instructed, so in spiritual regeneration by baptism, there is required some one who will receive the baptized from the holy font, and nurture, inform, and instruct him in those things which belong to the faith, to the Christian life, and to the Divine worship. At the same time, this is not of necessity to the Sacrament, but only in order to preserve and utilize the grace therein given. Among Catholick Christians, the godparents may reasonably presume that the child is duly instructed by its natural parents, and unless they know or suspect the contrary, they are not themselves bound to undertake its instruction.

LI. Since no man can attain salvation unless he be incorporated into Christ, and baptism, whereby we are made members of His Body, is the means of this incorporation, all men must needs receive it. To all men it is said, Ye must be born again, for except a man be born again of water and of the Spirit, he can neither enter into nor see the Kingdom of God. We must be baptized into Christ, and so putting on Christ be made the children of God. Even before Christ's Advent, men could not be saved but by being made members of Him, for neither is there salvation in any other, for there is none other Name under heaven given among men, whereby we must be saved. And so before His Advent men were incorporated into Christ by faith of His

Advent, then future, the seal of which faith was Circumcision. Before the institution of Circumcision, by faith alone, along with the offering of sacrifices, by which the old fathers made profession of their faith, were men incorporated into Christ. Although, therefore, the Sacrament of Baptism was not always necessary to salvation, faith, of which Baptism is the Sacrament, always was.

LII. The baptized are renewed according to the Spirit, but the flesh remains subject to the oldness of sin. And so they who are begotten after the flesh inherit and retain original sin until freed therefrom by being born again after the Spirit. Those who are sanctified from the womb receive grace cleansing them from original sin, but they do not receive character configuring them to Christ. In order to receive this they must receive Baptism.

LIII. Those who, despising this sacrament, receive it neither in reality nor by desire, cannot be saved, because neither sacramentally nor mentally are they incorporated into Christ, through whom alone is salvation. But those who, being by death or other accident prevented from receiving the sacrament, desire to do so, this desire arising from a faith which worketh by love, God, whose power is not bound down by visible sacraments, interiorly sanctifies, and saves.

LIV. Infants are to be baptized immediately. 1. As incapable of instruction or more perfect conversion. 2. For the peril of death, seeing that in them the lack of baptism cannot be amended by desire. The baptism of adults is to be deferred. 1. To prove their sincerity. 2. For examination of their faith and morals. 3. For their further instruction. 4. Until the solemn times for baptism, to wit, at Easter and Whitsunday. But it is not to be deferred. 1. If they are fully instructed and fit therefor, as in the case of Philip and the eunuch, and Peter and Cornelius. 2. Or in case of infirmity, siege, persecution, shipwreck, or other peril of death.

LV. Baptism is not to be bestowed on sinners who have a will to sin, and a purpose of persevering and continuing therein. Such men cannot be united to Christ, for what fellowship hath righteousness with unrighteousness. There would be, moreover, a want of correspondence between the sign and the thing signified. No man possessing free will can begin a new life till he repent of the old. And, as S. Augustine says, He who, without thee, created thee, will not without thee, justify thee. But on those who are sinners by reason of past guilt, its stain and penalty, the Sacrament is certainly to be conferred, for thereto was it instituted, that is, in order to their removal.

LVI. No satisfactory work is to be enjoined on the baptized, because they are by their baptism made partakers of the Passion and Death of Christ, which was a full, perfect, sufficient, and superabundant satisfaction for all sin. The punishment of the Head was satisfactory for the sins of all the members of His Body, as the punishment of one member may be satisfactory for the sins of another member. As S. Augustine says, The grace of Baptism requires neither sigh nor groan, but faith alone.

LVII. Confession to a Priest is not required before Baptism. 1. Because it belongs to the sacrament of Penance, which must be preceded by Baptism, it being the gate of the Sacraments. 2. Because in Penance the Priest looses from sins, and binds to works of satisfaction which are not to be enjoined in Baptism. He does not need remission of his sins by the power of the keys, to whom all his sins are remitted in Baptism. All that is required is such a general confession of his sins before God as is implied in his desire to begin a new life, and the general confession which the Ritual of the Church demands, that he renounces Satan and all his pomps. If of devotion he wish to confess his sins, his confession is to be heard, but no work of satisfaction is to be imposed.

LVIII. There must be intention on the part of the baptized, and this intention he professes when, according to the Ritual of the Church, he demands his baptism. There must be also faith on the part of the baptized, in order to his reception of grace, the ultimate effect of baptism; but character may be impressed without it. This faith he professes in the creed which he recites. His faith as to the Sacrament may be defective, but it is sufficient that he have a general intention to receive Baptism as Christ instituted, and as the Church has handed down the same.

LIX. Infants are to be baptized. 1. Because of their original sin, which their liability to pain and death proves them to possess. 2. In order that, being nurtured from childhood in the religion of Christ, they may the more steadily persevere therein, according to the proverb, Train up a child in the way he should go, and when he is old, he will not depart from it.

LX. The processes of spiritual regeneration are reflected in those of carnal generation. As the child living within the mother's womb derives its nourishment, not from its own exertions but from hers, so a baptised child without the use of reason, is, as it were, within the womb of the Church its mother, and is nourished by her acts, not by its own, seeing that it can neither believe with its heart unto righteousness, nor confess with its mouth unto salvation.

LXI. The children of unbelievers, who have not yet attained the use of reason, are not to be baptised against the will of their parents, under whose care they are placed by the Natural Law, any more than a person is to be baptised against his own will. But after such children have the power of free will, they may rightly be admonished and induced to receive baptism.

LXII. The baptism of a pregnant mother does not redound to the child *in utero*, because it is of necessity to baptism that the body be in some way washed with water. The life of the mother is not to be taken to save the child's, for we must not do evil that good may come; but if the mother be dead and the child alive, her body is to be opened in order that the child may be baptized. Unless in cases of great danger complete birth is to be waited for before baptism. When danger is very imminent the head may be baptised, and if so, the baptism will not be iterated. Where this cannot be, any other part of the body may be baptised; but in this case the baptism will be conditionally iterated.

LXIII. Those born insane are to be regarded as infants without the use of reason, and baptized; those who, born sane, have since lost their sanity, are even while insane to be baptised, if during their sanity they have had the intention, but not otherwise. And so with those who have lucid intervals, although in this case when danger is not imminent, a lucid interval is to be waited for, that the Sacrament may be received with more devotion. The same rules apply to those who are sleeping. In imminent danger they are to be baptised, if they have while waking had the intention, and not otherwise; when danger is not imminent, their baptism is to be delayed till they awake.

LXIV. Since all sin pertains to the oldness of the life to which a man by his baptism dies, it is clear that all sins are taken away by baptism; and not only the *guilt* of all sins, but the liability to punishment by reason of them, since by baptism there is communicated to a man the merit of the passion of Christ, which merit belongs to the baptised just as if he himself had suffered and died. But the passion of Christ was a sufficient and superabundant satisfaction for the sins of all men; consequently, it is as if every baptised person satisfied for his own sins, by bearing the punishment due to them. This he does by being made a member of that Body of which He who suffered and satisfied is the Head.

Water, by its washing properties, signifies the washing away of sin; by its cooling properties it signifies also the freedom from punishment which is effected in Baptism; and by its clearness the grace and virtues therein conferred.

LXV. But although baptism has the power of taking away the penalties of the present life, yet it does not take them away in the present life or until the Resurrection: 1. because it is meet that the incorporated members of the one Body should suffer and die as did its Head, should like Him bear the cross, and so with Him, obtain the crown; 2. lest men should come to baptism, in order to avoid the sufferings of the present life, instead of in order to gain the glories of the life eternal.

LXVI. In original sin the person first infected the nature, and thereafter the nature infected the person. Christ repairs first the defects of the person, and afterwards those of the nature. The guilt of original sin and its punishment, the loss of the sight of God, so far as regards the person, He takes away immediately by Baptism, along with the pains of hell; but the pains of the present life, as hunger, thirst, pain, death and the like—defects of nature—He does not take away until the general reparation of human nature in its glorious resurrection.

LXVII. Being incorporated into, and made members of that Body of which Christ is the Head, we receive in our baptism of the fulness of His grace and virtues. We are by Him illuminated in order to a knowledge of the truth, and impregnated with grace in order to a fruitfulness in good works.

LXVIII. Their Mother, the Church, says S. Augustine, accommodates to her babes the feet of others that they may come, the hearts of others that they may believe, the ears of others that they may hear, the understanding of others that they may be instructed, and the tongues of others that they may confess. And so they believe, not by their own act, but by the faith of the Church which is communicated to them. And by virtue of this faith there is conferred on them grace and virtues, acts of which they will be capable of when they attain the use of free will, as those who are asleep are capable when they awake.

LXIX. The guilt and punishment of sin closed against man the gate of the Kingdom of Heaven. These being wholly taken away by Baptism, that Sacrament is said to open the gate of the Kingdom of Heaven.

LXX. Baptism produces the effect for which it was specially ordained— that is, regeneration to the spiritual life, *equally in all infants* who approach not with their own faith, but with the faith of the Church. Adults receive grace according to their devotion and dispositions; but the least baptismal grace is sufficient to destroy all the sins which it finds in the soul. Extraordinary effects of baptism, as bodily healing, or destruction of the law of sin in the members, are *miraculously* bestowed by God irrespective of disposition.

LXXI. Fiction—which consists: 1, in unbelief; 2, or in scorn; 3, or in non-observance of the ritual of the Church; 4, or in indevotion—hinders the effect of baptism; which, however, emerges when the fiction is removed by penitence. But the sins subsequent to the baptism and previous to the penitence are taken away, not by Baptism, but by penitence, and therefore not as to their whole *reatus*.

LXXII. Since our faith and the faith of the old fathers is one and the same, and all things happened unto them for figures, it is clear that circumcision, which was a protestation of their faith, was preparatory to and prefigurative of Baptism, which is the Sacrament of ours. Abraham was the first of them who received the promise of the Messiah, and was the first to separate himself from the society of the unbelieving, and so it was meet that in his person circumcision should be instituted. By his time, too, the traditional faith had become weak; natural reason had become darkened by the increase of carnal concupiscence, even to sins against nature; and multitudes were given to idolatry. As original sin is transmitted not by the mother, but by the father, so circumcision was ordained—not for women, but for men. Circumcision was fitly performed *in membro generationis*—1, because it was a sign of the faith whereby Abraham believed that Christ would be born of his seed; 2, because it was for a remedy of original sin which is transmitted by the act of generation; 3, because it was ordained for the diminution of carnal concupiscence, which chiefly reigns therein. In circumcision as in baptism, grace was conferred as to its effects, but not in virtue of the circumcision, but in virtue of that faith of which circumcision was the sign. They received remission indeed—not only of original, but of actual sin, but not of all punishment as in Baptism.

LXXIII. Baptism being the Sacrament of the Christian faith, instruction in that faith is necessary in order to its reception. And so, before Baptism comes Catechism, as the Lord commanded, saying, Go and teach all nations, baptising them: and in like manner as the life of grace pre-supposes the life of rational nature. There are four kinds of instruction—1, one converting to the faith; and this belongs not only to every preacher, but also to every believing man: 2, instruction in the rudiments of the faith; which belongs to the sacred ministers, and especially to priests: 3, instruction in the conversation of the Christian life; which belongs to god-parents: 4, instruction in the profounder mysteries of the faith, and in the perfection of the Christian Life, which *ex officio* pertains to Bishops.

3. THE SACRAMENT OF CONFIRMATION.

LXXIV. THE Sacraments of the New Law are ordained to produce certain special effects of grace. Wherever a special effect of grace is contemplated, there is ordained a special sacrament to be its vehicle. In those things which are bodily, and are approached by the senses, there is a likeness to those things which are spiritual, and are approached by the intellect. From a knowledge of the details of the bodily life, we arrive at a knowledge of the details of the the spiritual life. The processes of nature run parallel to the processes of grace. In the natural life, besides generation, there is increase, strength, and arrival at a perfect age: in the supernatural or spiritual life, besides regeneration which takes place in baptism, there is increase, strength, and arrival at a perfect age; and to accomplish this special effect of grace, there is ordained a special Sacrament, viz., Confirmation.

LXXV. Christ instituted this Sacrament, not by exhibition of it, but by promise. *It is expedient for you that I go away; for if I go not away the Comforter will not come to you, but if I depart I will send Him to you.* There is given in this Sacrament the plenitude of the Holy Ghost, which was not to be given before the resurrection and ascension of Christ, as S. John relates, *The Holy Ghost was not yet given, because that Jesus was not yet glorified.*

LXXVI. The Sacraments of the New Law are prefigured in those of the Old. As S. Paul taught the Corinthians, the fathers *were all baptized unto Moses, in the cloud and in the sea, and did all eat the same spiritual meat, and did all drink the same spiritual drink.* But Confirmation, being the sacrament of the fulness of grace, could have nothing corresponding to it under the Old Testament, for, as the Apostle wrote to the Hebrews, the law made nothing perfect.

LXXVII. All the Sacraments are in some way necessary to salvation; but there are some without which there is no salvation, others which co-operate to the perfection of salvation. And in this way Confirmation is of necessity to salvation, although there may be salvation without it, when it is not omitted from neglect or contempt.

LXXVIII. Those who receive Confirmation, the sacrament of the fulness of grace, are conformed to Christ, who, from the first instant of His Conception, was full of grace and truth; and the fulness of whose grace was declared at His Baptism by the descent upon Him of the Holy Ghost in a bodily form.

LXXIX. The fit matter of this sacrament is oil mixed with balsam. The oil signifies the fulness of the Holy Ghost; the balsam signifies the odour of sanctity, whereby we are unto God a sweet savour of Christ.

Christ, of the excellence of His power, conferred this sacrament without the matter of chrism, using, however, sensible signs—as fire, of which oil is the matter and fomenter; and tongues, which have communicative power, as has also balsam. The Apostles also sometimes conferred this sacrament without chrism, but then with certain sensible and miraculous signs, as S. Peter says, *As I began to speak the Holy Ghost fell on them as on us at the beginning.* When these signs were absent they commonly used chrism.

Baptism is a sacrament of absolute necessity, and so its matter is found everywhere; not so in Confirmation, which is not of so great necessity.

The whole sanctifying power of the sacraments is derived from Christ. The matter of Baptism and of the Eucharist received its aptitude for the conveyance of grace from the touch of the adorable Humanity of the Lord's Body. Hence it is not of necessity to these Sacraments that their matter be first blessed; their benediction is simply an additional solemnity. But Christ did not use visible unctions, not to prejudice His invisible unction with the oil of gladness above His fellows; and so the matter of Confirmation is, previous to its use, blessed by a Bishop, who, as such, personates Christ in the Church.

LXXX. The words—I sign thee with the sign of the cross, and I confirm thee with the chrism of salvation, in the name of the Father, the Son, and the Holy Ghost. Amen.—are the fitting form of this sacrament, as expressing— 1, the cause conferring the plenitude of spiritual strength, which is the Holy Trinity; 2, the spiritual strength communicated in order to salvation, by the sacrament of visible matter; 3, the sign of the Captain of our salvation, in which He triumphed, given to His soldier, viz. the cross, in the strength of which he is to go forth and fight and conquer.

LXXXI. In every sacrament which is not iterated, and Confirmation is one of them, there is impressed *character*, which is a certain spiritual power ordained in order to certain sacred actions, in the case of Confirmation to fight against the enemies of the Faith, whether visible or invisible, corporeal or spiritual. The character of Confirmation of necessity presupposes the baptismal character. As no man can come to a perfect age unless he have first been born, so no man can be confirmed unless he have first been baptized. If he be, he receives nothing, and must be again confirmed after baptism.

LXXXII. The Divine power is not bound to sacraments; and so spiritual strength publicly to confess and to shed one's blood for the faith of Christ, may be and has been conferred on men without the Sacrament of Confirmation, as also the remission of sins without the Sacrament of Baptism. In either case there must be desire of the Sacrament; and this in the latter case even before the reception of baptism.

LXXXIII. The Apostles were baptized either with John's baptism, as some think; or, as is more probable, with the baptism of Christ before their reception of the Holy Ghost at Pentecost.

Those who heard the preaching of Peter received the *effect* of Confirmation before they received the *Sacrament of Baptism*, but they had previously received the *effect* of baptism, viz., justification. And this accounts for Peter commanding them to be baptized, even after they had received the gift of tongues.

LXXXIV. The grace of Confirmation is a grace *gratum faciens*. The first effect of grace *gratum faciens* is the remission of sins; but it has also other effects, and among them increase and establishment in righteousness.

LXXXV. This Sacrament is given to confirm what it finds: and so it ought not to be given to those who have not grace: and therefore neither to the unbaptized nor to adults in mortal sin. By this Sacrament the effects both of penitence and baptism are perfected; and by the grace therein conferred the penitent obtains a fuller remission of his sin. If an adult be in mortal sin, of which he is unconscious, or if he be not perfectly contrite, he will, so that he approach unfeignedly, receive remission of his sin.

LXXXVI. As it is of the intention of nature to bring all who are corporally born to a perfect age, although this is sometimes hindered by reason of the corruptibility of the body, and prevented by death, so much the more is it of the intention of God to bring all men to perfection. The soul to which pertains both spiritual birth and spiritual perfection of age is immortal, and may in time of bodily old age be spiritually born, even as it may in bodily boyhood or youth attain to perfection of spiritual age. Age is not venerable merely by reason of many years. In earthly warfare a place is denied to slaves and women, old men and boys; the spiritual warfare is open to persons of every condition, and age, and sex. Many women have warred with the souls of men, nay, sometimes with even a greater fortitude.

LXXXVII. This Sacrament is to be conferred even on those who are about to die, not as necessary by reason of the perils of the present life, or that they would be damned if they went hence without it, but lest they should suffer loss. They who in the next world are to attain to greater glory, must in this world obtain greater grace.

LXXXVIII. The confirmed are signed with the sign of the cross on the forehead; 1. as on an evident place, it being seldom covered; 2, as the seat of shame; and 3, of fear; two chief hindrances to the confession of the name of Christ. For fear the forehead grows pale, while it reddens for shame.

LXXXIX. As young soldiers need captains and centurions from whom to learn the manœuvres of war, so do the young athletes of the faith need godparents, persons of experience, by whom they may be instructed in the use of the arms which Confirmation has bestowed; and 2, as a sign that they are yet feeble and infirm in the spiritual life. These contract the same affinity as in baptism, and their relationship is an impediment to marriage in the same way.

XC. This function is reserved to Bishops; 1, as the successors of the Apostles, whose exclusive privilege it was; 2, because it belongs to the generals to enrol the soldiers who are to fight under their banners, and be subject to their orders; 3, because it belongs to the master to give the finishing touches to the picture or statue which the workman has begun or blocked out. Ye, says the Apostle to the Corinthians, are the Temple of God, and the Spirit of God dwelleth in you. And every one of us is become, in our baptism, a living Epistle, written with the Blood of Jesus, whereby may be known and read of all men His goodness, His orders, His promises, and His powers. To be authentick, this epistle must be signed. And so in Confirmation, the Bishop signs with the Seal of the Holy Ghost the letter which has been written by the priest, his secretary.

XCI. It is most fitting, albeit not of strict necessity, that both he who gives and he who receives this Sacrament be fasting. Chrism may be consecrated at any time, but ordinarily and most fittingly on Maundy Thursday; 1, in readiness for (in the ancient Church) the solemn baptism on Easter eve; 2, because it was fitting to prepare the matter of the Sacraments the same day on which was instituted the Blessed Sacrament, to which all the rest have reference, and in order to which they were all instituted and ordained.

4. THE SACRAMENT OF THE EUCHARIST.

XCII. S has been said, the spiritual life is conformed to the bodily life. Now, as in the bodily life there is required *generation*, whereby man receives life; and *increase*, whereby he is brought to perfection, so also is there required *aliment*, whereby he is preserved in life. In like manner in the spiritual life, as there is Baptism, which is spiritual generation, and Confirmation, which is spiritual increase, so is there also the Sacrament of the Eucharist, which is spiritual aliment.

XCIII. As a man, although composed of many members, or a house, although composed of many parts, is yet one; so the spiritual refection of the Eucharist, although, being composed of spiritual meat and spiritual drink, it is materially more than one, yet formally and perfectively it is one, as befits the Sacrament of Ecclesiastical Unity.

XCIV. In this Sacrament two things are to be considered; 1, the Sacrament itself: 2, the reality *(res)* of the Sacrament. The *res* of this Sacrament is the unity of the Mystical Body, without which there cannot be salvation, any more than in the flood without the Ark of Noah. But the *res* of a Sacrament may be had by desire before actual reception of the Sacrament, as has been shewn in the case of baptism. Here, however, occurs a difference. Baptism is the beginning or principle of the spiritual life, and the gateway of the Sacraments; whereas the Eucharist is, as it were, the consummation of the spiritual life and the end of all the Sacraments; for the sanctifications effected by all the other Sacraments, are but just so many preparations for either receiving or consecrating the Eucharist. And so the reception of Baptism is necessary to the beginning of, and the reception of the Eucharist to the consummation of, the spiritual life. Again, a man is baptized in order to the Eucharist; and as by the faith of their mother the Church, baptised infants believe, so by Her intention do they *desire to receive* the Eucharist, and consequently they receive its *res* before they actually receive the Sacrament itself, or even if they are by death or otherwise necessarily prevented from ever actually receiving it. But unbaptized infants cannot, like unbaptized adults, desire baptism, and so neither can they desire the Eucharist, and by desire receive its *res*, the unity of the Mystical Body. The reception then, of the Eucharist, actually, or by desire, is *necessary to salvation*, but not in the same way as is the reception of baptism.

One is, in a manner, made partaker of Christ's Flesh and Blood, when made a Member of His Body by Baptism.

XCV. Bodily aliment is converted into the substance of him who is nourished thereby; but the spiritual aliment converts man into Itself. St. Augustine says, as if repeating the words of Christ: Thou wilt not change Me into thee, as the food of thy body, but thou thyself will be changed into Me.

XCVI. Baptism is the Sacrament of Faith, which is the foundation of the spiritual life; the Eucharist is the Sacrament of Charity, which is the bond of perfection.

XCVII. In respect of the past, and as commemorative of the Lord's Passion, the Eucharist is called a *Sacrifice*. 2. In respect of the present, and as effective of ecclesiastical unity—that is union with Christ as the Head, and with each other as the members of the One Body—it is called a *Communion* by the Latins, and by the Greeks a *Synaxis*; in respect of the future, and as prefigurative of the fruition of God, which will be in our fatherland, it is called a *Viaticum*, as affording us a way of going thither. In respect of this, also, it is called a *Eucharist*, that is, good grace; because the grace of God is life eternal, or because It really contains Christ, who is full of grace. It is called also in Greek *Metalepsis*, that is, an *Assumption*, because we thereby assume the Deity of the Son.

XCVIII. Since He was about to remove from men's eyes that Body which He had assumed, and to carry It beyond the stars, it was necessary that He should leave It to man under a Sacramental species, that That might ever and continually be worshipped in a mystery, which was once offered for a price. 2. It was necessary that during all time there should exist among men a representation of the Lord's Passion. Under the Old Testament there was the Sacrifice of the Paschal Lamb, to which, since Christ our Passover is sacrificed for us, succeeded under the New Testament the Sacrifice of the Eucharist. The one is rememorative of the past as the other was prefigurative of the future passion. 3. In order the more deeply to grave it on the memories, and impress it on the hearts of His disciples, Christ instituted the Sacrifice of the Eucharist on the very eve of His Passion.

XCIX. In the Sacrament of the Eucharist there is, 1. That which is *Sacramentum only:* viz., bread and wine; 2. That which is *res and Sacramentum:* viz., the True Body of Christ; 3. That which is *res only;* viz., the effect of this Sacrament. 1. Of the first, the principal figure was Melchizedeck's oblation of bread and wine. 2. All the Sacrifices of the Old Law were figures of the second, and more especially the Sacrifice of Expiation, which was the most solemn of all. 3. Of the third, the principal figure was the Manna, angels' food, as says the Wisdom of Solomon, sent from heaven, prepared without man's labour, able to content every man's delight, and agreeing to every taste. 4. But the Paschal Lamb was a figure of all the three. 1. As eaten with unleavened bread. 2. As slain by the whole multitude of the children of Israel on the fourteenth day of the month. 3. As protecting, by its blood, the children of Israel from the destroying Angel, and causing their deliverance from the bondage of Egypt.

C. The matter of the Sacrament of the Eucharist, as it was instituted by Christ, is bread and wine. And this for many reasons. 1. As signifying the use of this Sacrament, which is manducation. 2. As signifying the Passion of Christ, in which His Blood was separated from His Body. 3. As signifying its effect on the bodies and souls of men, the Blood under the species of wine being offered for the salvation of the soul which is in the blood. 4. As signifying the unity of the one Church composed of many members, as the bread is made of many grains, and the wine extracted from many grapes.

Although wheat and wine do not grow in all countries, yet in all countries they may easily be procured. Without the one, the other may not be consecrated, because both are necessary to the perfection of the Sacrament.

Among the errors as to the matter of this Sacrament were those:—1. Of the Artotyritae, who offered bread and cheese, saying the oblations of the first men were of the fruits of the earth and of sheep. 2. Of the Cataphrygians and Pepuzians, who offered a cake made of flour, moistened with the blood of an infant, which they obtained by puncturing its whole body with minute wounds. 3. Of the Aquarians, who offered water only, under pretence of sobriety.

CI. Wheaten bread, as the most strengthening, the most commonly used, and that which, as it is believed, Christ used, is the proper matter of the Eucharist? Although it may be fermented according to the custom of some churches, yet it is more fitting that it be unleavened. 1. As agreeable to the institution of Christ, who instituted this Sacrament on the first day of unleavened bread, on which day ought no leaven to be found in any house of the Jews. 2. Because it is the Sacrament of the Body of Christ, which was conceived without corruption. 3. As signifying the required sincerity of the faithful. Christ, our Passover, is sacrificed for us, therefore let us keep the feast, not with the *leaven* of malice and wickedness, but with the *unleavened bread* of sincerity and truth. Unleavened bread is the use of the Latin churches; leavened bread the use of the Greek, to signify that the Word of the Father was clothed with flesh, as the leaven is mingled with flour. A Latin priest would sin who celebrated with leavened, a Greek priest would equally sin who celebrated with unleavened bread, both as perverting the rites of their respective churches.

CII. Wine of the grape, and that only, is the proper matter of this Sacrament: 1, of the institution of Christ; 2, as signifying spiritual joy; for wine maketh glad the heart of man. As with bread so with wine, if either be totally corrupt, there is no sacrament; if partially corrupt, there is a sacrament, but he sins who celebrates it.

CIII. With the wine a little water ought to be mingled: 1, as agreeable to the institution of Christ, for it is the probable belief that the Lord instituted this sacrament in wine mingled with water, according to the custom of the country; 2, to represent the blood and water that flowed from His Side in the

Passion on the Cross; 3, to signify the union in and by means of the Eucharist, of Christian people with Christ, they being symbolised by the water; 4, to signify Its ultimate effect, an entrance to Eternal Life. But the admixture of the water is not of necessity, any more than is that which is signified thereby, the reception of the faithful, necessary to the perfection of the Sacrament, which consists in the consecration of the matter. But a very small quantity of water is to be added, especially if the wine be weak, lest its species should be destroyed, and itself rendered unfit to be the matter of the Sacrament.

CIV. That the True Body and Blood of Christ are in this Sacrament, can be comprehended neither by the senses, nor by the intellect, but by faith only, resting on the Divine authority. It is meet that it should be so: 1, in order to the perfection of the New Law. The Sacrifices of the Old Law contained the true Sacrifice of the Passion of Christ only in figure. The Law had a shadow of good things to come, but not the very image of the things. So the Sacrifice of the New Law was instituted by Christ to contain something more —namely, to contain Him who suffered, Christ Himself, not only in signification or figure, but in reality and in truth. And so this Sacrament, which really contains Christ Himself, is perfective of all the other Sacraments in which is participated the virtue of Christ. 2. As belonging to the charity of Christ, of which charity it was that for us men, and for our salvation, He assumed a True Body of our Nature. As this Sacrament is the support of our hope, so is it the sign of charity. 3. As belonging to the perfection of faith, which, as it concerns the Divinity of Christ, so does it also concern His Humanity. Faith is of the invisible. As Christ exhibited His Divinity to us invisibly, so does He also in an invisible manner exhibit to us His Flesh.

Some, not attending to this, have laid down that the Body and Blood of Christ are not in this Sacrament, save in sign; a heresy to be abhorred as contrary to the words of Christ. Berengarius, the first author of this error, was ultimately compelled to recant, and confess the true faith.

CV. Some have said, that after consecration, the substance of bread and wine remain. But this cannot be, for—1, it would be contrary to the reality of the Sacrament; 2, it would be contrary to the *form*, This is My Body, which in that case ought rather to be, Here is My Body; 3, it would be contrary to Its due veneration, if any created substance remained which could not be worshipped with *Latria*, the supreme worship due only to the Creator; 4, it would be contrary to the rite of the Church, according to which the Body of Christ may not be received after ordinary food. Did the substance of bread and wine remain, it would not be lawful to receive one Consecrated Host after another had been already consumed. The position is to be avoided as heretical.

CVI. After Consecration the substance of the bread or wine is—1, not resolved into the prejacent matter; neither, 2, is it annihilated; but, 3, it is converted into the true Body of Christ. By conversion, and in no other way, does the Body of Christ begin to be in the Eucharist. This conversion is not similar to natural conversions, but is altogether supernatural, and effected by the power of God alone. It is rightly called by the special name of Transubstantiation.

CVII. Faith is not contrary to sense, but concerns that to which the senses cannot attain.

CVIII. As is apparent to the senses, all the accidents of bread and wine remain. Christ willed to set forth His Body and Blood for the reception of the faithful in the Eucharist, under the species of bread and wine—1, that the merit of men's faith might be increased: 2, occasion of ridicule taken away from the unbelieving, as well as, 3, that abhorrence which would be excited in all by the eating of human flesh.

CIX. Since the whole substance of the bread is converted into the whole substance of the Body of Christ, the substantial form of the bread does not remain.

CX. The conversion is effected in an instant. It is effected by the words of Christ, which are pronounced by the Priest; and the last instant of pronouncing the words is the first instant in which the Body of Christ is in the Sacrament.

CXI. It is of the Catholick faith that Whole Christ is in this Sacrament. 1. His Body and Blood *ex vi* of the Sacrament, under the species respectively of bread and wine, as declared in either case by the formal words. 2. His Soul and Divinity by natural concomitance with both.

Since the Divinity never laid down that Body which It had assumed, wherever the Body of Christ is there must of necessity be His Divinity also.

Christ's Soul was really separated from His Body by death. And so, if, during the Three Days, this Sacrament had been celebrated, there would not have been present the Soul of Christ, either *ex vi* of the Sacrament, or by real concomitance. But Christ being risen from the dead dieth no more, and so His Soul is always really united to His Body, and evermore present therewith.

There is contained under the species of bread, not only the flesh of Christ, but His bones and sinews, &c., for the form declares not, This is My flesh, but, This is My Body.

CXII. Although under the species of bread the Body of Christ only, and under the species of wine the Blood of Christ only, is contained *ex vi* of the Sacrament, yet it is most certainly to be held as *de fide* that under each species is contained Whole Christ, God and Man, Body, Soul and Divinity, by virtue of concomitance. For instance, under the species of bread is contained not only the Body of Christ, *ex vi* of the Sacrament, but His Blood also as concomitant therewith. In like manner, under the species of wine is contained not only the Blood of Christ, *ex vi* of the Sacrament, but His Body also as concomitant therewith: as has been shewn above with regard to His Soul and Divinity, present with both Body and Blood by real concomitance.

Had the Eucharist been celebrated during the Three Days of the Passion, when Christ's Body and Blood lay separate, there would have been contained under the species of Bread, His Body only, and not His Blood; and under the species of wine His Blood only, and not His Body.

At no time was His Divinity separated from Body or Blood, and so at no time would His Divinity have been absent under either species of Bread or Wine.

CXIII. Whole Christ is in the Host while It remains entire, and in every part of It when It is broken.

CXIV. In no way is the Body of Christ *locally*, in this Sacrament, that is, as in a place.

CXV. Whole Christ remains in the Sacrament so long as the sacramental *species* remains.

CXVI. By no bodily eye may Christ be seen as He is in this Sacrament; neither by the sense nor imagination may He be perceived, but by the intellect alone, which is called the eye of the spirit, and by that supernatural process of it which is called Faith. The Blessed, whether angels or men, see Christ sacramentally present in the Eucharist, as they see all things else which are supernatural, by virtue of that brightness of the Divine Intellect which they share.

Visions of Flesh or Blood or a Body, are miraculous apparitions, and not realities contained under the sacramental species.

CXVII. The accidents of bread and wine remain after consecration, not as in a subject, in the substance of bread and wine which does not remain, neither in a substantial form which does not remain, and if it did could not be their subject—but without a subject. God, who is the first cause of substance and accident, can, by His own Infinite Power, preserve in being accidents from which he has substracted the substance, by which the accidents were preserved in being as by their proper cause. As also He can, without natural causes, produce other effects of natural causes, as, for instance, He formed a human body in a Virgin's womb without seed of man. Nothing prevents one thing being ordained according to a common law of nature, and another being ordained according to a special privilege of grace.

CXVIII. The sacramental species retaining the same being *(esse)* after consecration as before, may after consecration be corrupted as they might have been before it. And albeit they have no matter, yet dimensive quantity taking the place of matter, there may, as is evident to the senses, be something generated from them, as ashes if they be burned, worms if they putrefy, or dust if they be ground to a powder. As therefore, the sacramental species may be converted into any substance which is generated from them, they may be converted into the human body; or in other words, they have power of nourishment. The sacramental species may be broken, as is evident by reason of their dimensive quantity. It must be so, because, 1, their substance, not being there, cannot be broken, and 2, the Body of Christ cannot be broken; because, 1, It is incorruptible, and impassible, and 2, It exists entire under every particle.

A liquid may be mixed with the consecrated wine in such quantity as to destroy the species of wine, in which case the Blood of Christ ceases to be contained under it. If mixed in a quantity so small as not to vary the species, the Presence is not removed.

CXIX. The Sacrament of the Eucharist differs from other Sacraments in two things. 1. In that it is perfected by *consecration* of the matter, while they are perfected by *use* of the consecrated matter. 2. In that in the other Sacraments the consecration of the matter consists only in a benediction, from which the matter consecrated receives instrumentally a spiritual virtue, which proceeds, by means of the minister, who is the animated instrument, to instruments which are inanimate; whereas in this Sacrament the consecration of the matter consists in a miraculous conversion of substance, which can be effected by God alone. And hence the minister, in the effecting of this Sacrament, has no act to perform other than the pronouncing of the words. ii. Since the form should be fitted to the reality, the form of this Sacrament. differs from the forms of other Sacraments in two things. 1. They import a use of matter as in baptism and confirmation; this imports only the consecration of the matter, which consists in the transubstantiation, namely, when it is said, This is My Body, or, This is the Chalice of My Blood. 2. They are pronounced in the person of the minister, or by way of exercising an act, as when it is said, I baptize thee, or, I confirm thee; or by way of command, as in the Sacrament of Order it is said, Receive power, &c.; or by way of deprecation, as in the Sacrament of Extreme Unction it is said, By this unction and our intercession, &c. But the form of this Sacrament is pronounced as in the person of Christ Himself who is speaking, that it may be given to understand that the minister, in the effecting of this Sacrament, does nothing save pronounce the Words of Christ.

CXX. A priest pronouncing these words and these only, with intention, will truly consecrate, but will grievously sin, as not observing the rite of the Church. The formal words, and they only, are of necessity. The Canon of the Mass has not been the same at all times, and is not the same in every place. The formal words pronounced in the person of Christ, have an instrumental virtue, effective of the transubstantiation. They effect what they signify.

CXXI. The most Holy Sacrament of the Eucharist confers grace, because it contains Christ, who is the fount and origin of all grace. Grace and truth came by Jesus Christ. Coming visibly into the world, He conferred on the world the life of grace; coming sacramentally to man, He operates in man the life of grace.   1. Whoso eateth Me shall live because of Me.   2. That which the Passion of Christ did in the world, this Sacrament of Christ does in a man. From His Side continually flows the Water and the Blood.   3. As material meat and drink in the bodily life, so Sacramental meat and drink in the spiritual life sustains, increases, repairs, and delights.   As He said: My Flesh is meat indeed, and My Blood is drink indeed. 4. As the bread is made of many grains, and the wine expressed from many grapes, so by this Sacrament are many Christians made One in the One Christ.   "O Sacrament of Piety," says S. Augustine, "O sign of Unity, O bond of Charity!" 5. S. John Damascene compares this Sacrament to the live coal taken from off the altar which Esaias saw. For as a coal is not simple wood, but united to fire, so is the bread of communion not simple bread, but united to divinity. 6. An effect of the Eucharist, as containing Christ and as representing His Passion, is the attainment of life eternal. He that eateth of this bread shall live for ever.   7. Christ's Passion is a sufficient cause of our future glory, but it does not immediately introduce us thereto. We must first suffer with Him if we will hereafter be glorified with Him. In like manner this Sacrament does not immediately introduce us to glory, but gives us the power of arriving thereat at the last. Whence it is called a *Viaticum*, a provision for the way. For a figure of this it is written that Elijah ate and drank and walked in the strength of that meat forty days and forty nights unto Horeb, the Mount of God. 8. The Eucharist has power to remit all sins whatsoever, even mortal sins, supposing that he who receives It is not conscious of them, and approaches with affection, reverence, and devotion. 9. But he who has on his conscience mortal sin, cannot receive spiritual nourishment, seeing he is not spiritually alive. An unworthy reception works injury rather than benefit. 10. Nourishment is necessary to restore to the body that which it daily loses by the action of the natural heat. Spiritually there is a daily loss by reason of venial sins arising from the heat of concupiscence, which minishes the fervour of charity. This loss is supplied by the nourishment of the Eucharist, which operates to the remission of venial sins. 11. The whole pains of sin are not destroyed by reception of the Eucharist. They are diminished or partially remitted in proportion to the fervour and devotion of the receiver; for in satisfaction regard is had rather to the affections of the offerer, than to the quantity of his oblation. 12. Sin is the death of the soul. Death is prevented—i. by food and medicine, which are ordained against internal corruptions; ii. by arms which are ordained against external assaults. The Holy Eucharist, supplying both, strengthens man's soul, repels the attacks of demons, and so preserves him from future sins. 13. But although it is a preservation from sin, it does not take from man the possibility of sinning, which remains so long as he retains the freedom of his will. 14. Although the Eucharist is not directly ordained to the diminution of the *fomes*, it does, however, diminish it inasmuch as it increases charity. 15. The effect of the Eucharist is not only the increase of habitual grace, but also a certain actual spiritual sweetness, which is destroyed when a man communicates with distractions which amount to venial sin. 16. But the increase of habitual grace is not hindered by past venial sins, nay, more, it is infused into the soul even where there is no actual devotion, and even where there is venial sin committed at the time.

CXXII. The Eucharist is at once a Sacrament and a Sacrifice. As a Sacrament it is received, as a Sacrifice it is offered. As a sacrifice it represents the Passion of Christ, whereby He offered Himself a sacrifice to God: as a sacrament it conveys invisible grace under a visible species. It profits those who receive it, and that both as it is a sacrament and as it is a sacrifice; those who do not sacramentally receive it, it profits also, but only as it is a sacrifice.

CXXIII. As in the Eucharist there is to be considered, not only, 1, the Sacramentum, but also, 2, its effect—so are there two modes of its reception. The one perfect, whereby one so receives the Sacramentum as to receive also its effect. The other imperfect, whereby one indeed receives the Sacramentum, but is by some impediment hindered from receiving its effect; or, on the other hand, whereby one indeed receives the effect, that is, union with Christ, but is precluded from receiving it by means of the Sacramentum its ordinary vehicle. The first is called, 1, Sacramental Manducation, the second, 2, Spiritual Manducation.

CXXIV. In the Eucharist is contained Christ Himself, not indeed under His own, but under the sacramental species. The angels spiritually manducate Christ under His own species; in as much as they are united to Him by the fruition of perfect charity and manifest vision (which bread we look forward to in our fatherland), and not by faith, as we are now united to Him. But to men alone, not to angels, it belongs spiritually to manducate Christ as contained in the Eucharist, under the sacramental species. In this sense we are to understand the saying that to man it is given to eat the Bread of Angels.

CXXV. So long as the species remain, so long does the Body of Christ remain under them. Now the species remains as long as the substance of bread would have remained, had it been present: in a receiver, so long as it remains undigested by the natural heat; and this whether the receiver be just or unjust. An unjust man sacramentally manducates Christ, as well as a just man, otherwise, how could he eating and drinking unworthily, eat and drink judgment to himself? The opinion that the Body of Christ was not received even sacramentally by sinners, but that so soon as the Sacrament touched their lips, so soon did Christ cease to be contained under the sacramental species, is erroneous. It proceeded from ignorance of the distinction between corporal and spiritual manducation. Even if a mouse or a dog manducate a consecrated Host, the substance of the Body of Christ does not cease to be under the species, so long as the species remains, that is, so long as the substance of bread would have remained, had it been present. Neither do these exceptions derogate from the dignity of the Body of Christ, who willed to be crucified by sinners, and was so crucified without detriment thereto; more especially since He is received not under His own, but under sacramental species.

CXXVI. In this Sacrament, as in others, that which is *sacramentum* is a sign of that which is *res sacramenti*. But the *res* of this Sacrament is twofold. One which is signified and contained, viz., Christ Himself; the other, which is signified but not contained, viz., the Mystical Body of Christ, which is the Society of the Saints, that is, the fellowship of holy persons. Whoso, therefore, receives this Sacrament, signifies thereby that he is united to Christ, and incorporated with His Members, which he cannot be, unless by faith informed with charity. But such faith cannot co-exist with mortal sin; and so a person receiving in mortal sin, enacts a falsehood, and incurs the crime of sacrilege, as the violator of a Sacrament. Whoso eateth and drinketh unworthily, eateth and drinketh judgment, that is, damnation to himself.

CXXVII. True, this Sacrament is a spiritual medicine, but the same medicine will not be for the patient's good at all stages of his sickness. What will profit him whom the fever has left, will injure him in whom the fever remains. Baptism and Penance are, as it were, purgative medicines, exhibited to take away the fever of sin: the Eucharist is a strengthening medicine, not given save to those who have been freed therefrom.

CXXVIII. One may be unconscious of sin, 1, by one's own's fault, as by ignorance of the law, for *ignorantia juris non excusat;* or, 2, by ignorance of fact, which does excuse. A thief, ignorant that theft is a mortal sin, is an instance of the former; a person taking the property of his neighbour, in the belief that it is his own, is an instance of the latter. Again, one may be unconscious of sin, 3, by his own fault, not having sufficiently examined himself, for Let a man examine himself and so let him eat; or, 4, without his fault, as when he has indeed sorrowed, but not been sufficiently contrite. For no man has perfect certitude of the completeness of his contrition; it is sufficient that he find within himself the evident signs thereof, viz., sorrow for the past and a purpose of amendment for the future; 5, similarly, if a sin be totally forgotten, general contrition is sufficient for its deletion.

CXXIX. Infidelity and blasphemy, as sins committed directly against Christ's divinity, are more grievous than unworthy receptions of His Sacramental Body. And so, 2, were the injuries inflicted upon Him by Judas and the Jews, both because they were directed against His Natural Body, and, 3 were done with intention to hurt Him. 4. For this last reason, one who threw the Sacrament to dogs would sin more grievously than one who received it in mortal sin.

Still his sin is similar in kind to that of him who betrayed Jesus, and of those who slew Him.

S. Jerome says in one of his epistles, What hast thou to do with a woman who waitest on thy God at the Altar? Say, O priest, say, O clerk, how canst thou kiss the Son of God with the same lips with which thou hast kissed the lips of an harlot? With Judas, thou betrayest the Son of Man with a kiss.

CXXX. To open and manifest sinners, known to be such either by public reputation or by conviction before any tribunal, religious or secular, the Holy Communion is to be denied, even if they demand it. This, as St. Cyprian says, both the Divine Majesty and Evangelical Discipline, severally exact.

But to secret sinners who request it, this right of every baptized person cannot be denied. But a priest who is aware of his sin ought privately to admonish him, or in general terms to warn all such not to approach the Lord's Table before repenting them of their sins, and being reconciled to the Church. For after penance and reconciliation the Holy Communion is not to be denied, even to public sinners, and more especially *in articulo mortis*.

CXXXI. Quanquam nocturna pollutio quam nullum mortale crimen praecessit vel causa : vit, non impediat necessario a sacramenti sumptione : deceret tamen sic dispositum abstinere.

CXXXII. Only mortal sin hinders *secundum se* the reception of the Eucharist, but by virtue of the Church's prohibition previous eating or drinking is a bar thereto. And this for a threefold reason. 1. For the honour of the Sacrament. 2. To signify that Christ, who is the *res* of this Sacrament, and His charity, ought to be first established in our hearts. Seek ye first the Kingdom of God. 3. To avoid all peril of vomiting and drunkenness, which sometimes result from an inordinate use of meat or drink. As St. Paul complained to the Corinthians: one is hungry, and another is drunken.

From this general rule are excepted the infirm, who are at once to be communicated, even after food, if they are in peril of death, lest they should depart without the Viaticum. For necessity has no law. Throughout the whole world, says S. Augustine, is the custom observed of receiving the Body of Christ fasting.

CXXXIII. Some begin their day at noon, some at sunset, and some at midnight ; the Roman Church begins its day from midnight, and so if after midnight one take anything by way of meat or drink he may not on the same day receive the Eucharist.

CXXXIV. Not all who want the use of reason are to be hindered from reception of the Eucharist, but those only who have never had the use of reason ; those who in the beginning enjoyed the use of reason, and were afterwards deprived of it, and who during a lucid interval have exhibited devotion to, and desire of the Sacrament, are to have It administered to them *in articulo mortis*, if there be no peril of expulsion or irreverence.

The Sacrament is not to be given to children till they attain such use of reason as to conceive a devotion thereto. The Greeks administer the Communion to infants, the Latins do not. Yet do not the infants thereby suffer loss, for, as S. Augustine teaches, every one of the faithful is made a partaker of the Lord's Body and Blood *spiritually*, when in his baptism he is made a member of the Body of Christ.

CXXXV. As to frequent reception of the Eucharist two things have to be considered. 1, One *ex parte* of the Sacrament itself, whose virtue is salutary to all men. And so it is useful daily to receive It, that man may daily receive Its fruit. As S. Ambrose says in his Book of the Sacraments. If as often as the Blood of Christ is poured forth, It is poured forth for the remission of sin, I ought always to receive ; I, who am always sinning, ought to have always a medicine. 2. In another way it is to be considered *ex parte* of the receiver, of whom it is required that he approach with great devotion and reverence. And so if every man found himself daily prepared it would be laudable that he should daily receive. And so, S. Augustine, saying, Receive daily that It may profit thee daily, adds, So live that thou mayest merit daily to receive. But since oftentimes in many men there occur impediments not a few to this devotion, by reason of indisposition of body or soul, it is not useful to all men daily to approach this Sacrament, but as often as each finds himself prepared. Hence, in his Book of Ecclesiastical Dogmas, he says, Daily to receive the Communion of the Eucharist, I neither praise nor blame.

CXXXVI. By the Sacrament of Baptism, a man is configurated to the death of Christ, receiving in himself the *character* of Christ, and so as Christ died but once, ought a man to be but once baptized. But in the Eucharist a man receives, not the *character* of Christ, but Christ Himself, whose virtue endureth for ever. This virtue man daily needs, and so may daily receive. 2. A man may be but once carnally born, and so may be but once spiritually born again. A man daily receives natural food, and so may daily receive supernatural food. Give us this day our Daily Bread. 3. The Paschal Lamb, as the principal figure of the Passion of Christ, who died once, was slain but once a year. The Manna, a type of the Eucharist, as It is our spiritual food and sustenance, was given to the people in the desert, day by day.

CXXXVII. There are present to the soul of the devout Communicant two feelings—1, one of love ; 2, the other, of reverential, or as it is theologically termed, filial fear. The one urges him daily to receive, the other sometimes to abstain. Receiving and abstaining, each alike does honour to his Lord. There was in this no difference between Zaccheus and the Centurion. The one joyfully received Jesus Christ; the other said, Lord I am not worthy that Thou shouldest enter beneath my roof. But Love and Hope, to which the Scripture is alway provoking us, are to be preferred to Fear. And so when Peter said, Depart from me for I am a sinful man, O Lord; Jesus answered, Fear not.

CXXXVIII. According to her estate at divers times, diverse statutes have emanated from the Church with regard to frequency of communion. For in the Primitive Church, while there flourished a great devotion to the Christian Faith, it was ordained that the faithful should daily communicate. Pope Anacletus says, The Consecration accomplished, let all communicate who will avoid the censures of the church, for so have the Apostles ordained, and so holds the Holy Roman Church. But afterwards, when the fervour of men's faith was lessened, Pope Fabian decreed that all should, if not more frequently, communicate at least thrice in the year, namely, at Easter, Pentecost, and Christmas. Still later, when iniquity had abundantly increased and the love of many had waxed cold, Innocent III., commanded that all of either sex should, at least once a year, and that at Easter, reverently receive the Sacrament, unless they should, by the counsel of their own priest, be induced for some reasonable cause to abstain for a season. It is advised in the Book of Ecclesiastical Dogmas that men should communicate on all Lord's Days.

CXXXIX. Since at least spiritual reception of the Eucharist is necessary to salvation, and it includes a purpose of receiving the Sacrament, which purpose would be vain were it not accomplished when opportunity permitted, it is clear that not only by precept of the church, but by command of Christ, who said, Do this in commemoration of Me, men are bound to receive the Eucharist. Wholly, therefore, to abstain therefrom on pretence of humility, is not true humility, which requires obedience. The centurion said, Lord I am not worthy that Thou shouldest enter under my roof; but he had never been commanded so to receive Christ.

CXL. In order to the perfection of the Sacrament, reception of both the Body and the Blood is necessary: and so the priest, to whom it belongs to consecrate and complete the Sacrament, must in no case receive the Body without the Blood. But to avoid all peril of irreverence, which is likely to occur chiefly with the Precious Blood, it is a prudent custom observed in many churches for the people to be communicated with the Body only, the Priest alone receiving Christ under both species.

The perfection of this Sacrament consists, not in its use by the faithful, but in the consecration of the matter; and so the reception by the faithful under one species only in no way derogates from the perfection of the Sacrament, when the consecrating priest receives under both, thereby completing the Sacrifice. Neither do any hereby suffer loss, seeing that, 1, in the person of all the priest offers and receives the Blood; and, 2, that under either species there is contained Whole Christ.

CXLI. Christ, whose custom it was to be the first to observe those ordinances which he commanded others to observe, in like manner as He willed to be Himself baptized before He imposed that Sacrament upon others, so did He first receive His own Body and Blood, and thereafter deliver them to be received by His disciples. He was, as S. Jerome says, at once Host and Banquet. *Ipse Conviva et Convivium.* As S. Paul taught the Hebrews— For as much as the children are partakers of Flesh and Blood, He also Himself likewise took part of the same.

> Rex sedet in cœna,
> Turba cinctus duodena,
> Se tenet in Manibus,
> Se cibat Ipse Cibus.

CXLII. The effect of this Sacrament is not only an increase of habitual grace, but also an actual delectation of spiritual sweetness. The first He needed not; but the second He received; and so He said, With desire I have desired to eat this Passover with you.

CXLIII. Although Judas merited to be deprived of the Sacrament by reason of his malice, yet the Lord delivered to him His Body and Blood, thereby to teach the Prelates of the Church to separate no men from their communion, whose sin is secret, without an accuser, and without evident proof; for although the iniquity of Judas was known to Christ, as He was God, yet it was not yet known to Him in the way common to mere men.

CXLIV. Christ, at divers times before His passion, assumed the four gifts of a glorified body, viz., subtility in His Nativity, when He issued from the closed womb of the Virgin ; agility when He walked dryshod on the sea ; brightness, in the Transfiguration ; impassibility, in the Supper, when He gave His Body to His disciples to eat. Now, it is manifest that the Body of Christ which was seen by His disciples under Its own proper species, was the same true Body as was received by them under the Sacramental species. But that Body as It was seen under Its own proper species, was not impassible, seeing It was ready prepared for the Passion, and so neither was the same Body of Christ which was received under the Sacramental species, impassible. But what was in Itself passible, was under the Sacramental species in an impassible mode, in like manner as what was in Itself visible, was there invisibly.

CXLV. Since the same Christ who was on the cross would have been in the Sacrament, had It been reserved during the time of His death, He would under the Sacramental species have sorrowed, died, and done aught else which pertained to Him as regarded Himself; but those things which had also relation to extrinsic bodies or agents, could only be attributed to Him as existing under His own proper species ; as, for instance, to be laughed at, spitted on, crucified, scourged, and the like.

>Pixide servato poteris sociare dolorem,
>Innatum, sed non illatus convenit Illi.

CXLVI. Under the species of bread is the Body of Christ *ex vi of the Consecration:* and in like manner under the species of wine is His Blood. Now, when the Blood of Christ is not separated from His Body, the Blood of Christ is under the species of bread along with His Body, *by real concomitance*, and in like manner His Body under the species of wine along with His Blood. But if, during the time of the Passion of Christ, when the Blood of Christ was separated from His Body, the Sacrament had been consecrated, there would have been under the species of bread His Body only, and under the species of wine His Blood alone. So also with regard to His Soul, It is now contained under both species, *of real concomitance*, with His Body and with His Blood present respectively under each ; but then It would have been present under neither, being separated from both.

But never at any time was His Divinity separated from either Body or Blood, and so It would always have been present with each existing respectively under Its several species.

CXLVII. As to a baptized person is given power to receive this Sacrament, so on one ordained priest is conferred the power of consecrating It in the person of Christ. By his ordination he is placed in the grade of those to whom it was said by the Lord, Do this for My Commemoration. It is, therefore, a function proper to a priest to consecrate the Body and Blood of the Lord on the altar of God.

CXLVIII. A holy laic is indeed united to Christ by a spiritual union by faith and charity, but not by sacramental power; and so may not by the use of the proper form and matter, consecrate the Sacrament. He has, indeed, a spiritual priesthood, but it is for the offering of *spiritual sacrifices*. As David says in the 51st Psalm: The Sacrifice of God is a troubled spirit; and S. Paul to the Romans: Present your bodies a living sacrifice, holy and acceptable unto God, which is your reasonable service; and S. Peter to the elect strangers: Ye are an holy priesthood, to offer up spiritual sacrifices.

CXLIX. Several priests may at one and the same time consecrate the same host, pronouncing at one and the same time the same formal words, and with the same intention.

It is a custom in some churches for newly ordained Priests to be concelebrants with the ordaining Bishop. Nor does this derogate from the unity of the action which is done in the person of Christ, since they, albeit many, are one in Him.

CL. The dispensation of the Body of Christ belongs to the Priest for three reasons—1, because he consecrates in the person of Christ, and as Christ consecrated His Body, so did He also Himself give It to be received; 2, as the divinely appointed *medius* between God and the people. As it belongs to him to offer to God the people's gifts, so does it also belong to him to deliver to the people those gifts divinely sanctified. 3, By reason of reverence, the Eucharist is touched by nothing which has not been previously consecrated, as the corporal, the chalice, and the Priest's hands.

The Deacon, as of kin to the sacerdotal order, in a manner shares the Priest's office. He dispenses the Blood, but not the Body, save in case of necessity, and at the command of the Bishop or Priest. And this, 1, because the Blood of Christ is contained in a vessel, and so is not touched by Its dispenser, as is the Sacred Body; 2, because the Blood signifies the redemption derived from Christ to the people represented by the water wherewith the wine is mingled: and the deacon stands midway between the priest and the people.

CLI. The Eucharist is not only a Sacrament, but also a Sacrifice. Now, whosoever offers sacrifice ought to be partaker of the sacrifice, since the outward sacrifice which is offered, is a sign of the inward sacrifice whereby one offers himself to God.

In like manner, he who dispenses the Sacrifice to the people thereby declares himself to be a dispenser of Divine things, whereof he ought himself to be first a partaker. As often, therefore, as a priest offers, he must receive the Eucharist in Its integrity, under both species.

CLII. Wicked Priests may consecrate the Eucharist, seeing they consecrate, not in their own persons, but in the person of Christ. And a consecration is neither better nor worse, effected by a holy or a wicked Priest, since neither consecrate in virtue of their own merits, but by the Word of God, and the power of the Holy Ghost. So also with regard to all prayers offered by the Priest in the person of the whole Church, and that whether in the mass, or in the Ecclesiastical offices. But of course the *private* prayers of a holy Priest are more fruitful and efficacious in proportion to his holiness.

CLIII. It is one thing not to have, another not to have rightly; just as it is one thing not to give or receive, another not to give or receive rightly. Now consecration of the Eucharist is an act which depends on the power of order: and so, whosoever is ordained has power to consecrate a valid Eucharist, under which is contained the True Body and Blood of Jesus Christ. Those who, while within the Church, have, in their ordination to the priesthood, received power to consecrate, do indeed *rightly possess* that power, but may not *rightly use* it, when by heresy, or schism, or excommunication, they have been separated from the Church. Those who, while so separated, have been ordained, neither rightly possess nor may rightly use this power. But *both possess* it, and so on their return to the unity of the Church, neither are re-ordained.

Those who exercise this power which they either do not *rightly possess* or may not *rightly use*, sin; and obtain not the fruit of their outward sacrifice, which is the inward and spiritual sacrifice. The sinner receives the Body of Christ *sacramentally* indeed, but *not spiritually*.

A separated priest consecrates in the person of Christ, by power of order; but certain prayers he says in the person of the whole Church, and such prayers, he being separated from her Unity, have no efficacy.

Moreover, a degraded priest can consecrate the Sacrament, seeing he does not thereby lose his sacerdotal *character*, which is indelible.

Those who receive the Sacraments from, or hear the Masses of excommunicated, heretical, or schismatic priests, separated by sentence of the Church from her communion, are thereby made partakers with them in their sins.

But the Sacrament consecrated by them is to be adored; and, if reserved, may be received at the hands of a lawful priest.

One is not to hear the Mass of a concubinary priest, known so to be of common notoriety, or by conviction, or by confession.

CLIV. Since every one ought to use the grace committed to him, at all fitting seasons and convenient opportunities, a priest may not, even although he have no cure of souls, wholly abstain from consecrating, but is bound to celebrate, at least, on all festivals, and chiefly on those on which Christ's faithful are wont to communicate.

CLV. For two reasons is the celebration of the Eucharist said to be an immolation of Christ. 1, As S. Augustine says, images are wont to be called by the names of those things of which they are the images, as when one sees a picture on the wall, one says, That is Cicero, or That is Sallust. Now the celebration of the Eucharist is a representative image of the Passion of Christ, which is His true immolation. And so the celebration of this Sacrament is said to be an immolation of Christ. 2, As regards the effect of the passion of Christ, seeing we are by means of the Eucharist made partakers of the fruits of the Lord's passion. As to the first mode, Christ may be said to have been immolated even in the figures of the Old Testament; as is said, for instance, in the Apocalypse, Whose Names are not written in the book of life of the Lamb slain from the foundation of the world. But as to the second mode, it is peculiar to this Sacrament. In the words of S. Augustine, Christ, who was in Himself immolated *once*, is yet *daily immolated* in the Sacrament.

CLVI. Because we daily need the fruit of the Lord's passion, by reason of our daily defects, this Sacrament is regularly offered daily in the Church.

And so the Lord teaches us to pray, Give us this day our daily bread; and S. Augustine, Receive daily, that it may daily profit thee.

As the Lord's Passion was celebrated from the third to the ninth hour, so during that part of the day is the solemn celebration of this Sacrament in the Church.

CLVII. When the truth comes, the figure ceases. Now the Eucharist is a figure of the passion; and so on that one day in the year on which there is a remembrance made thereof as it was really enacted once for all, there is no celebration. But that the Church be not on that day without the fruit of the Passion exhibited to us by this Sacrament, there is reserved to be received thereon, the Body of Christ consecrated on the preceding day. The Blood is not reserved, to avoid risk of accident; and also because the Blood is more especially the Image of the Lord's Passion.

This is the Good Friday Mass of the Presanctified.

CLVIII. On Christmas Day there are three celebrations, by reason of the threefold Nativity of Christ. 1, whereof one is eternal, and to us hidden. And so one Mass is sung in the night with this Introit, The Lord said unto Me, Thou art My Son, this day have I begotten Thee. 2, Another is temporal, but spiritual; that, namely, whereby Christ the Day-Star arises in our hearts. And so a second Mass is sung at dawn, with this Introit, To-day, and on us shall the Light shine. 3, The third Nativity of Christ is both temporal and corporal; that, namely, whereby He visibly proceeded from the Virginal Womb, clad in our flesh. And so a third Mass is sung in the bright light of day, with this Introit, Unto us a Child is born.

CLIX. The Eucharist is celebrated, on feast-days, at the third hour, when Christ was crucified by the tongues of the Jews, and when the Holy Ghost descended upon the disciples. On common days at the sixth hour, when Christ was crucified by the hands of the soldiers. And on fast-days, at the ninth hour, when, crying with a loud voice, He gave up the Ghost.

CLX. The house which contains the altar on which is offered the Sacrifice of the Eucharist signifies the Church, and is called a Church. It is consecrated—1, to represent the sanctification which the Church has attained by the Passion of Christ; as well, 2, as to signify the sanctity which is required of those who receive this Sacrament. A Church is never consecrated without an altar: but an altar may be consecrated without a Church; and the Eucharist, if celebrated in an unconsecrated Church, should be celebrated on a portable altar, consecrated by a Bishop, and containing relicks of the Saints or Martyrs whose life is hid with Christ in God.

Churches, altars, vessels, corporals, and other like inanimate creatures are consecrated, not as susceptive of grace, but as thereby rendered more meet for the Divine Worship.

The altar signifies Christ Himself, and so should be of stone, as it is said of Him: That rock was Christ. He lay, moreover, in a sepulchre hewn out of the rock. Wooden chalices are canonically forbidden, by reason of their porosity, and those made of glass, by reason of their fragility. Brass and copper are likewise inadmissible, as corrupting the wine. They must be made of either gold or silver, or at least of tin.

Corporals must be made of undyed linen, and not of silk, as representing the clean linen clothes in which the Body of Jesus was laid. They ought to be blessed by the Bishop.

Consecrated churches and altars, chalices and corporals, are of course not of necessity to the validity of the Eucharist, which requires only (1) the proper matter, with (2) the proper formal words (3), pronounced by a priest, (4) with due intention; but he sins grievously who celebrates without these, as not observing the ritual of the Church.

CLXI. Because in this Sacrament is comprehended the whole mystery of our salvation, it is celebrated with a solemnity far above the other Sacraments. Since it is written, Keep thy feet when thou goest into the house of God; and again, Before prayer, prepare thy soul; so before the celebration of this mystery, there is a preparation in order to the right performance of those things which follow. And of this preparation the first part is the Divine praise, contained in the Introit, according to the words of the Psalm—Whoso offereth Me thanks and praise, he honoureth Me, and to him that ordereth his conversation right, will I shew the salvation of God. The Introit is frequently taken from the Psalms, or at least sung along with a psalm, for, as Dionysius declares—the Psalms comprehend by way of praise whatsoever is contained in Holy Scripture. 2. The second part contains a commemoration of our present misery, when mercy is besought by saying Kyrie eleison three times for the person of the Father, Christe eleison three times for the person of the

Son; and again, Kyrie eleison three times for the person of the Holy Ghost. Kyrie eleison is said three times against our threefold misery of ignorance, guilt, and punishment, or to signify the mutual relations of the Persons. 3. The third part commemorates the celestial glory to which we tend after the present life and misery, by singing Gloria in excelsis Deo. This is sung on feasts on which the celestial glory is commemorated, but omitted in penitential offices, to which belongs the commemoration of the present misery. 4. The fourth part contains the prayers which the priest makes for the people, that they may be worthy of so great mysteries.

Secondly, There is, by way of preparation, an instruction of the faithful people, because this Sacrament is the mystery of the Faith. This instruction consists in the doctrine of the Prophets and Apostles, which is read in the Church by the Readers and Subdeacons. After this lection there is sung by the choir the Gradual, which signifies the progress of life, and the Alleluia, which signifies spiritual exultation, or the Tract in penitential offices, which signifies spiritual lamentation; for one or other of these ought to result in the people from the foresaid doctrine. The people are, then, perfectly instructed by the doctrine of Christ contained in the Gospel, which is read by the chief of the ministers, namely, by the Deacons. And because we believe Christ as the Faith of God so, the Gospel read, there is sung the Symbol of our Faith, in which the people declare themselves to assent by faith to the doctrine of Christ. The symbol is sung on Feasts, of which there is mention made therein, as on the feasts of Christ and the Blessed Virgin and the Apostles, and other like holidays.

And so, when the people have been prepared and instructed, they approach the celebration of the mystery, which is both offered as a sacrifice, and consecrated and received as a sacrament. In it is observed—1, the oblation; 2, the consecration of the matter; and 3, Its reception. As to the oblation, two things are done—1, the praise of the people in singing the offertory, whereby is signified the gladness of the offerers; and the prayer of the priest, who intreats that the offering of the people be accepted of God even as David said: As for me, in the uprightness of mine heart, I have willingly offered all these things; and now have I seen with joy Thy people, which are present here, to offer willingly unto Thee. And thereafter he prayed, saying, Keep this for ever in the imagination of the thoughts of the heart of Thy people. Then as to the consecration, which is wrought by supernatural power, the people are in the first place incited to devotion in the Preface, and admonished to lift up their hearts unto the Lord.

And then, the Preface finished, the people devoutly laud the Divinity of Christ, saying with the angels, Holy, Holy, Holy; and the Humanity, saying with the children, Blessed be He that cometh. Thereafter the Priest secretly commemorates, 1, those for whom the sacrifice is offered, namely, the Universal Church, and those who are set in authority, and those specially who offer, or for whom it is offered. 2. He commemorates the saints, whose patronage he implores for the foregoing, when he says: Communicating with and venerating the memory, &c. 3. Concluding his petition with the words—That this oblation may be, to those for whom it is offered, salvation. Then he comes to the Consecration itself, in which, 1, he first seeks to obtain the effect of the Consecration, Which oblation do Thou, O God, &c.; 2, he performs the Consecration by the Words of the Saviour, saying, Who the day before, &c.; 3, he excuses his presumption, pleading obedience to the command of Christ, Whence also mindful, &c.; 4, he begs that the sacrifice offered may be accepted of God, Upon which vouchsafe to look with apropitious, &c.; 5, he prays for the effect of this sacrifice and sacrament (1) in regard to the receivers, when he says, We most humbly beseech Thee, &c., and (2) in regard to the dead, who cannot now receive, when he says, Remember also, O Lord, &c. (3) and specially in regard to the priests themselves who offer, when he says, Also to us sinners, &c. Then he comes to the Reception of the Sacrament, and, i., he prepares the people to receive, 1, by the common prayer of the whole people, which is the Lord's prayer, in which we pray may be given us our daily bread; and also, 2, by the private prayer which the Priest specially offers for the people, when he says, Deliver us, O Lord, we beseech Thee, &c. ii. The people are prepared by the peace which is given, saying, The Lamb of God, &c.; for this, as has been said, is the sacrament of unity and peace. But in masses for the dead, in which the sacrifice is offered not for the present peace, but for the repose of the dead, the Peace is omitted. Then follows the receiving of the Sacrament, the priest first receiving, and then delivering It to others. Lastly, the whole celebration of the mass is brought to a close by thanksgiving, which is signified on the part of the people by the Post-Communion Chant, and on the part of the priest by his prayer of thank-offering, thus following the example of Jesus Christ and His Apostles, who sang a hymn after the celebration of the first Eucharist.

CLXII. Certain portions of the service are said by the choir; those, namely, which pertain to the people. Of these, some are begun by the priest who personates God, to signify that certain things come to the people of Divine revelation, as faith and celestial glory, and so the priest begins the Creed, the Symbol of the Faith, and the *Gloria in excelsis Deo.*

Other portions are said by the ministers, as the doctrine of the Old and New Testament; and this for a sign that by ministers sent from God this doctrine was announced to the people.

Other portions the priest alone pronounces, those namely which are proper to his office, which is, as the Apostle says, to offer gifts and prayers for the people. Among these are certain common prayers pertaining partly to himself, and partly to the people, and them he says publickly. The rest, as those regarding the Oblation and Consecration, pertain to himself alone, and so are said by him secretly. But before both he excites the attention of the people by saying, The Lord be with you, and awaits their assent, who say Amen.

The *secreta* also signify that during the Passion the disciples did not confess Christ save secretly.

CLXIII. There is no inconsistency in the priest asking of God that which he most certainly knows God will do, for Christ Himself prayed for His own glorifying, which He knew was determined aforehand of His Father. But the prayer, That It may become unto us the Body and Blood, &c., is not that the Consecration may be accomplished, but that the Consecrated may be fruitful to Its receivers.

CLXIV. When the priest prays, Command these things to be carried by the hand of Thy Holy Angel to Thine Altar on high, he does not ask, either that the sacramental *species* should be borne away to heaven, or the Very Body of Christ, which does not cease to be there; but he prays on behalf of the Mystical Body which is signified in this Sacrament, that the Angel assisting at the Divine Mysteries may present to God the prayers of priest and people; even as S. John, in the Revelation, saw him come and stand at the altar in heaven, having a golden censer, and there was given unto him much incense, that he should offer it with the prayers of all Saints upon the golden altar which was before the Throne, and the smoke of the incense, with the prayers of the Saints, ascended up before God out of the Angel's hand.

From this, moreover the mass (*missa*) derives its name: because, by the angel the priest sends (*mittit*) the prayers to God, as do the people by the priest; or else, because Christ is the sacrifice sent (*hostia missa*) by us to God. And so, at the end of the mass on festivals, the deacon lets the people depart, saying, *Ite, missa est, i.e.*, Go; the sacrifice has been sent to God by the hands of the angel, that it may be accepted of Him.

CLXV. The whole ceremonial which surrounds this Sacrament is founded on most fitting reasons, and has been ordained, either, 1, To represent the Passion of Christ; or, 2, In order to increase the reverence and devotion of the faithful members of His mystical Body.

CLXVI. The *washing of the priest's hands* during the celebration of the mass has been instituted, 1, Out of reverence to the sacrament; for we are not wont to handle aught of price with unwashen hands, and we may not approach so great a sacrament with hands even corporally unclean. Inasmuch as washing the extremities signifies cleansing even from the least sins, as Jesus said, He that is washed needeth not save to wash his feet, but is clean every whit. Such cleansing is required of all who approach this Sacrament.

And this, moreover, is signified by the Confession which is made before the introit of the mass. It was also prefigured by the washings of the priests, under the old Law. Aaron, and his sons, and their seed after them throughout their generations were, when they went into the Tabernacle of the Congregation, or when they came near to the Altar to minister, to burn offerings made by fire unto the Lord, to wash their hands and their feet in the laver of brass which was placed between the Tabernacle of the Congregation and the Altar. Under the New Law the priests' feet are not washed; the washing of his hands sufficing to signify perfect cleansing. To the hand, the organ of the organs, *organum organorum*, as it is called (3. *de animâ*) all works are attributed; and so David sings in the Psalms, I will wash mine hands in innocency, O Lord, and so will I go to Thine Altar.

CLXVII. The *use of Incense* is for two reasons. It is used—1, out of reverence, by its good odour to dispel any evil odour; 2, to represent and signify the effect of grace residing in Christ, and from Him the Head, derived, by means of His ministers, to us the Members of His Body, whereby, as says the Apostle to the Corinthians and to us, we are unto God a sweet savour of Christ. Thanks be to God who always maketh manifest the savour of His knowledge *by us* in every place.

And so the Altar, which signifies Christ, having been incensed on every side, all are incensed in their order.

CLXVIII. The priest uses *the Sign of the Cross*, to express the Passion of Christ, which terminated in the Cross. Now the Passion had several stages. There was—1, the Betrayal, which was enacted by God, Judas and the Jews. This is signified by the trine signation at the words—These ✠ gifts, these ✠ presents, these holy and ✠ unspotted sacrifices. 2. There was the Sale of Christ, which was performed by the Priests, the Scribes, and the Pharisees. This is signified by a second trine signation at the words—to be ✠ blessed ✠ approved ✠ ratified. It may be also to signify the price of thirty pieces of silver. There is added also a double signation at the words—That It may be to us the ✠ Body and ✠ Blood. This designates the two persons—Judas the Seller and Christ the Sold. 3. There was the foreshewing of the Passion made in the Supper. To signify this there are two signations, one made at the Consecration of the Body, the other made at the Consecration of the Blood, when there is said over each—He bless✠ed it. 4. There was the Passion itself, and so to represent the Five Wounds there is a fivefold signation at the words—a pure ✠ Host, an Ho✠ly Host, a Host ✠ Immaculate, the Ho✠ly Bread of Eternal Life, and the Chalice ✠ of Everlasting Salvation. 5. There is represented the extension of the Body, and the effusion of the Blood, and the fruit of the Passion by the trine signation at the words—That as many as shall partake at this Altar of the most Sacred ✠ Body, and ✠ Blood of Thy Son may be filled ✠ with all heavenly grace and blessing. 6. There is represented the threefold prayer which He made on the Cross. i. For His persecutors, in the words, Father, forgive them; ii., for deliverance from death, in the words, My God, My God, why hast Thou forsaken Me. iii. The third pertains to the attainment of glory, in the words, Father, into Thy Hands I commend My Spirit. To signify these there is a trine signation at the words—By whom, O Lord, Thou dost always create, sanc✠tify, quic✠ken, and ✠ bless. 7. There are represented the Three Hours during which He hung on the Cross, namely, from the sixth to the ninth hour. To signify them there is a trine signation at the words By ✠ whom, and with ✠ whom, and in ✠ whom. 8. The separation of Soul and Body is represented by the two subsequent crosses made—one beyond and the other in front of the chalice, at the words—be unto Thee, God the Father Al✠mighty in the unity of the Holy ✠ Ghost, all honour and glory. 9. The resurrection on the third day is represented by three crosses made at the words—The Peace of the Lord ✠ be al✠ways with ✠ you.

Briefly; the Consecration of this Sacrament, the acceptance of this Sacrifice, and the fruits thereof, proceed one and all from the virtue of the Cross of Christ; and so wherever there is mention made of any of these, the priest uses the sign of the cross.

CLXIX. When after the Consecration the priest *extends his arms*, he thereby signifies the extension of the Arms of Christ on the Cross.

In praying, also, he *lifts up his hands* to signify that his prayer is directed for the people to God; as it is written in the Lamentation of Jeremiah: Let us lift up our heart with our hands unto God in the heavens. And again, when Amalek came and fought with Israel in Rephidim, Moses stood on the top of the hill with the rod of God in his hand. And it came to pass, when Moses held up his hand, that Israel prevailed, and when he let down his hand Amalek prevailed.

He sometimes also *joins his hands* and *inclines* himself. This is the attitude of one who prays with simplicity and humility, and signifies the humility and obedience of Christ, out of the abundance of which He suffered.

After the Consecration he keeps the *thumb and index finger of his right hand*, with which he has touched the Consecrated Body of Christ, *joined*, out of reverence, lest any particle thereof should have adhered to them and suffer accident.

CLXX. The Priest *five times turns himself* to the people, to signify that the Lord five times manifested Himself on the day of His Resurrection.

He *salutes them seven times*, five times turning himself to them and twice not, as when before the Preface he says, The Lord be with you, and again, The Peace of the Lord be with you always. And this he does to signify the sevenfold graces of the Holy Ghost. The Bishop, celebrating on feast-days, says in the first salutation, Peace be unto you, for so said Jesus to His disciples after His Resurrection, and Him the Bishop principally personates.

CLXXI. The *Fraction of the Host* signifies three things—1, the division of the Body of Christ, which was made in the Passion; 2, the distinction of the Mystical Body according to its divers estates; 3, the distribution of those graces which proceed from the Passion of Christ.

CLXXII. According to Pope Sergius, the particle placed in the chalice shows forth the risen bodies of Christ, of the blessed Virgin, and of any other saints who may have their bodies in heaven; 2, the particle eaten designates those who are still walking on the earth, using the Sacraments, and ground down by sufferings, as the bread eaten by them is ground by their teeth; 3, the particle remaining on the Altar till the end of the mass is the Body in the Sepulchre; for even till the end of the world shall the bodies of the saints be in their sepulchres, their souls being, as the case may be, in purgatory or in heaven. This last rite, the reservation of a particle till the end of the mass, is not now observed, by reason of the peril attending it. But there remains the same signification of the particle, which is metrically expressed in the lines:

> Hostia dividitur in partes, tincta beatos
> Plenè, sicca notat vivos, servata sepultos.

CLXXIII. Of the Paschal Lamb, which was the principal figure of this Sacrament, it was commanded that there should not remain aught until the morning; and, inasmuch as the truth ought in some way to respond to its figure, so there ought not to be reserved till the morrow any part of the Consecrated Host from which the priest, ministers, and people have been communicated. Pope Clement ordered that the sacrifice should be offered on the Altar in such quantity as should suffice for the needs of the people; and that if any remained it should not be reserved till the morrow, but consumed by the diligence of the clergy, with fear and trembling.

There is, however, this difference between the Eucharist and its figure, the Paschal Lamb, that the one is received daily, the other was not. And so there ought to be other Hosts consecrated to be reserved for the sick, and these the Priest ought to have always by him in readiness, lest any one should die unhouselled.

CLXXIV. In solemn celebrations of the mass there ought to be present several persons. Pope Soter says that no priest should presume to celebrate a solemn mass, unless there be present two persons to respond to him, he himself being the third, because since he says in the plural numbers: The Lord be with you (Dominus *vobiscum*), Let us give thanks (Gratias *agamus*), and, Pray ye for me (*Orate* pro me), it is most plainly evident that there ought to be more than one person to answer to his salutation. But in private masses it suffices to have one minister, who, personating the whole Catholick people, in their place plurally respond to the priest.

CLXXV. Perils or defects may be—1, prevented by previous care ; or, 2, amended or remedied ; or, 3, at least repented of by him through whose negligence they have occurred.

CLXXVI. If a priest be overtaken by death or grievous infirmity *before the Consecration*, his place need not be supplied by another. But if this happens *after the Consecration has begun*—say, when the Body has been Consecrated, but before Consecration of the Blood, or even after both have been consecrated, the celebration of the mass must be completed by another. Nor is this diversity of persons inconsistent with the unity of the function, seeing we are all one in Christ.

CLXXVII. If a priest, after the Consecration is begun, remember that he has that day eaten or drunk somewhat, he is nevertheless to receive the Sacrament and so make perfect the Sacrifice, as by far the least of two evils ; any thing hindering the perfection of the sacrifice being an horrible sacrilege. In like manner, if he remember that he has committed some sin, he ought to repent with a purpose of confession and satisfaction, and so he will, not unworthily, but fruitfully receive the Sacrament.

Similarly, if he remember that he is lying under any excommunication, he ought to make a purpose of humbly seeking absolution, and so obtain absolution from the Invisible Pontiff Jesus Christ, in order that he may proceed with the Divine Mysteries.

But if he remember any of the foresaid impediments *before consecration*, I deem it safer, especially in the cases of eating and excommunication, that he leave off the mass he has begun, unless there be danger of grievous scandal.

CLXXVIII. If a *fly or spider fall into the chalice* before consecration, or if it be apprehended that there is *poison* mingled with the wine, it ought to be poured out, the chalice cleaned, and filled afresh.

But if the first accident occur *after* consecration, the animal should be carefully caught, diligently washed, then burnt, and its ashes, along with the water, poured down the drain in the *sacrarium*.

If it be apprehended that *poison is mingled* with the Blood, It is by no means to be received or given to others, lest the chalice of life should turn to death. It ought to be placed in a fitting vessel and reserved with the relicks.

But that the Sacrament may not remain imperfect, the priest will pour other wine into the chalice and resume from the Consecration of the Blood, and so perfect the Sacrifice, which is not complete till after Its reception in both kinds by the priest.

CLXXIX. If the priest, after the Consecration of the Body, but *before the Consecration* of the Blood, perceive that there is no wine or water in the chalice, he will at once supply it and Consecrate.

But if *after the words of Consecration* he perceive that the water is wanting, he ought nevertheless to proceed, because the mingling with water is not of necessity to the Sacrament. He, however, ought to be punished through whose negligence the defect has occurred.

In no case is water to be mingled with already consecrated wine.

If *after the words* of Consecration of the Wine, and *before reception* of the Body, he perceive that no wine has been placed in the Chalice, he ought, having first poured out the water, if there be any, to supply wine with water, and resume from the words of Consecration of the Blood.

But if he perceive this defect, *not until after* his reception of the Body, he ought to take another host and consecrate it along with the Blood. The reason of this is that in the Consecration of the Blood there are certain things said and done which have reference to the Body as well as to the Blood. Now the Body would not be present if already received, and so would arise an incongruity which would interfere with the order of the sacrifice. This second Host he is to receive along with the Blood, even notwithstanding his previous reception of the water which was by itself in the chalice; a non-fasting reception being a less evil than a sacramental imperfection.

CLXXX. If the priest remembers that he has *omitted words* which are *not of necessity* to the Sacrament, he is not to resume, and so alter the order of the sacrifice, but to proceed. But if the *omitted words are of necessity* to the Sacrament, as the form of Consecration, the form being as necessary in order to the Sacrament as is the matter, he is to resume from the form of Consecration, and reiterate all in order, so that the order of the Sacrifice be not changed.

CLXXXI. Omission of the Fraction, which is a significant act, but not of sacramental necessity, does not necessitate any reiteration.

CLXXXII. Any place on which has fallen a drop of the Precious Blood is to be scraped and washed, if a cloth the piece cut out and burnt, and the ashes and the ablutions to be taken by the priest, and placed under the altar, or poured down the drain in the *sacrarium*.

5. The Sacrament of Penance.

CLXXXIII. ENANCE, wherein the sinner, by what he says and does, shews that he has in his heart departed from sin, and wherein the priest, by what he says and does, signifies the work of God, who remits the sin, is a special sacrament.

CLXXXIV. That which in Penance is sacrament only is the external act, whether of the sinner repenting, or of the priest absolving; that which is both reality and sacrament *(res et sacramentum)* is the sinner's interior repentance; while that which is reality only, and not sacrament, is the remission of sin.

CLXXXV. The acts of the penitent constitute the proximate matter of this sacrament; the remote matter consists of his sins, which are not to be accepted, but detested and destroyed.

CLXXXVI. As the words and acts of the penitent are the matter, so the words and acts of the priest are the form in this sacrament, which consists not in the consecration of any matter, or in the use of any sanctified matter, but in the removal of its remote matter, to wit, the sinner's sins. As the Sacraments of the New Law effect what they figure, so ought their form to signify what they effect. Absolution from sins being the effect of penance, the proper form is—I absolve thee. Christ said to His disciples, Go teach all nations, baptizing them; and in virtue of these words His priests say—I baptize thee. He said also to Peter, Whatsoever thou shalt bind on earth shall be bound in heaven, and whatsoever thou shalt loose on earth shall be loosed in heaven; and in virtue of these words they likewise say—I absolve thee. Farther, words declaring his authority as, In the name of the Father, and of the Son, and of the Holy Ghost; or, By virtue of the Passion of Christ; or, By the Authority of God, not being determined by the words of Christ as in Baptism, are left to the judgment of the Priest.

CLXXXVII. Public absolutions, as in Prime, Compline, and the Communion, such as, Almighty God have mercy upon thee; or, God grant thee absolution and remission, are not sacramental, but are prayers ordained for the remission of venial sins. They are added to the Sacramental absolution to prevent the effect of that absolution being hindered on the part of the penitent.

CLXXXVIII. The imposition of hands in certain sacraments, as in Confirmation and Orders, is intended to designate a copious effect of grace. But the effect of Penance as of Baptism is the removal of sins, and so in neither is the laying on of hands of necessity.

CLXXXIX. The Sacrament of Penance is not absolutely necessary to salvation as is the Sacrament of Baptism, that is, it is not necessary for all, but for those only who are subject to sin; as medicine is not necessary save for the sick. As in the natural life a man needs generation, increase, and nourishment, although he may not need medicine, so in the spiritual life a man needs Baptism, Confirmation, and the Eucharist, although he may not need Penance. By Baptism he is received into the Ark of Christ's Church; Penance is his second plank after the shipwreck of sin. So S. Jerome.

CXC. Interior Penance, whereby one grieves for the sin committed, ought to last to the end of life, for by taking pleasure in, one renews past sin; but the external signs of penance need last, not during one's life, but only for a determinate period, according to the measure of one's sin. Penance as an act cannot possibly be continual, but as a habit it ought to be so, that is, one ought never to do anything contrary to penance whereby his habitual disposition thereto may be lessened or destroyed.

CXCI. Seeing that Charity once had, may by reason of the freedom of the will be lost, and seeing that the Divine Mercy exceeds the magnitude and multitude of all sins whatsoever, it is clear that penance may be oftentimes repeated. A person can be but once non-existent, and so can be but once born. A soul can be but once in original sin, and so can be but once baptized. But a person can be often sick, and so can be often healed. And a soul may often sin, and so may as oftentimes repent.

CXCII. That repentance which is in the sensitive appetite is a passion rather than a virtue; but that penitence which is in the will is a virtue, or an act of virtue. It is a special virtue whereby a man works in order to the destruction and detestation of past sin, inasmuch as it is an offence against God.

CXCIII. The penitent returns to God with a purpose of amendment, as does, 1, a servant to his lord. Behold, even as the eyes of servants look unto the hand of their masters, and as the eyes of a maiden unto the hand of her mistress, even so our eyes wait upon the Lord our God, until He have mercy upon us. 2. A son to his father. Father, I have sinned against heaven and before thee. 3. A wife to her husband. Thou hast played the harlot with many lovers, yet return again to me, saith the Lord.

CXCIV. Penitence is not a theological virtue, because it has not God for its object or matter; but it is allied to the theological virtues, inasmuch as it is accompanied by faith in the passion of Christ, whereby we are justified from sin, and by hope of pardon for, and hatred of, past sin, which hatred of sin pertains to charity.

CXCV. Penitence *as a passion* is a species of sorrow which resides in the concupiscible as its subject. *As a virtue* it is a species of justice, and has for its subject that appetite of the reason which is the will. Its proper act is a purpose of amending that which has been committed against God. Penitence is not in the memory, but presupposes it. Memory is apprehensive of the past, but penitence is not apprehensive, but appetitive.

CXCVI. The first act in penitence is the operation of God converting the heart. 2. The second is a motion of faith. 3. The third is a motion of servile fear, whereby one is dragged back from sin by a fear of its punishment. 4. The fourth is a motion of hope, whereby one, with the hope of obtaining pardon, makes a purpose of amendment. 5. The fifth is a motion of charity, whereby sin becomes displeasing by reason of itself, and not by reason of its punishment. 6. The sixth is a motion of filial fear, whereby, by reason of reverence, one voluntarily offers amends to God. And so any act of penitence proceeds from servile fear as its first motion, but from filial fear as its immediate and proximate principle.

CXCVII. In justification, along with the motion of the free will towards God and from sin, there is a remission of guilt and an infusion of grace, along with which are at the same time infused all virtues.

CXCVIII. To affirm that there is in this life any sin whereof one may not repent is erroneous, 1, as depriving man of the freedom of his will, which is flexible towards good as towards evil; 2, and as derogatory to the virtue of Divine grace, whereby the sinner's heart is moved to repentance.

CXCIX. Mortal sin proceeds from the aversion of man's will from God by its conversion to a commutable good; penitence consists in the re-conversion of the will to God, with detestation of the past, and a purpose of amendment for the future: and so it is impossible that mortal sin can be remitted to any one without penitence, that is, without the *virtue* of penitence. But God may remit sin without sacramental penitence, as in the case of the adulteress and the woman that was a sinner. There is this difference between God's grace and man's grace, that man's grace presupposes, whereas God's grace causes the conversion of the will.

CC. It is impossible that one sin can be remitted by penitence without another, 1, because no sin is remitted without grace, and every mortal sin is contrary to, and excludes grace; 2, because no mortal sin is remitted without true penitence, and it belongs to the very idea of penitence to desert all sin as against God; 3, because it would be contrary to the perfection of the mercy of God, whose works are perfect.

CCI. When, by the virtue of penitence, the guilt of sin is remitted to a man, there is remitted also the eternal punishment due therefor, but not necessarily and always the temporal punishment. The reason is this. In a mortal sin there is both, 1, an aversion from the Incommutable Good, and, 2, an inordinate conversion to a commutable good. The first deserves an eternal and infinite punishment, as a sin against an Eternal and Infinite God. But the second, being finite, does not deserve an eternal punishment, although, at the same time, being inordinate, it does deserve a punishment which is finite and temporal, it being but just that he who has indulged his will more than he ought should suffer somewhat against his will, and so an equality be preserved. Hence if there exist an inordinate conversion to a commutable good without an aversion from God, as is the case in venial sins, punishment is indeed due, but it will be temporal, and not eternal. When, therefore, by the grace of God, the guilt of sin is remitted, and the aversion of the soul from God removed, inasmuch as by grace the soul is re-united to God, there is at the same time taken away the liability *(reatus)* to eternal punishment, although a liability to temporal punishment may remain.

The aversion from God is the formal cause, the conversion to a created good the material cause of a mortal sin.

CCII. The Passion of Christ is a sufficient satisfaction for the punishment due to all sins, whether temporal or eternal; and a man is freed from liability to temporal punishment in proportion as he participates in the virtue of the Passion. In baptism participating wholly he is wholly freed from liability to even temporal punishment; but in Penance participating according to his disposition he is in like measure set free.

CCIII. There may, after the remission of guilt, remain in the soul certain dispositions (rather than habits) to sin, caused by previous acts of sin. These dispositions, or relics of sin, as they are called, are, however, both lessened and weakened, that they may not have dominion over a man. They occupy the same place with regard to Penance as the *fomes peccati* does with regard to Baptism.

CCIV. The power of the Keys being the form, while the acts of the penitent are the matter of this sacrament, the remission of sins, which is its effect, although it may not be without penitence as it is a virtue, is yet more principally to be attributed to penitence, as it is a Sacrament, that is, more to the acts of the priest than of the penitent.

CCV. In the justification of the ungodly there is, besides the infusion of grace and the remission of guilt, a motion of the free will toward God, which is faith with love, and another towards sin, which is penitence.

CCVI. Venial sins, which hinder man's affections from being readily set upon God, although they do not, like mortal sin, avert his soul from Him, do not require so perfect a penitence, but they must be repented of by a virtual displeasure and sorrow for having committed them. This will not suffice for the remission of mortal sins, which must be diligently recollected and individually detested.

CCVII. Venial sin is not destructive of habitual grace or charity, neither does it diminish it, but retards its action; and so for the remission of venial sin there is not necessarily required a fresh infusion of habitual grace or charity, but only a motion of the same—that is, an act of virtual penitence, either explicit or implicit.

CCVIII. The body may be stained in two ways—1, either by privation of somewhat which is necessary to its beauty of colour; 2, or by the presence of something which defiles it as mud or dust. The first corresponds to mortal sin staining the soul, which requires for its obliteration a fresh infusion of grace; the second to venial sin, which needs only for its removal an act proceeding from grace, which implies detestation of sin or reverence towards God, as a general confession—a beating of the breast, saying the Lord's Prayer, receiving Episcopal Benediction, or taking Holy Water. They are, of course, *a fortiori* remitted by means of any of the ordinances for infusion of fresh grace, as the Holy Eucharist, or any of the Sacraments of the New Law.

It follows that venial sins cannot be remitted without the remission of mortal sins, whose presence implies the absence of grace in the soul.

CCIX. Aversion from God and its consequences, loss of grace and liability to eternal punishment, are common to all mortal sins. And so S. James says, Whosoever shall offend in one point, he is guilty of all. But as regards inordinate conversion to a commutable and created good, mortal sins are diverse, and sometimes contrary. Hence a subsequent mortal sin does not cause previous mortal sins which have been abolished to return, otherwise a man by a sin of prodigality might be brought back to a disposition or habit of avarice, and so a contrary become the cause of its contrary, which is impossible.

The remission of past sins was a work of the mercy of God, and so cannot be made void by the subsequent sin of man. But sometimes the subsequent act of sin virtually contains the *reatus* of the previous sin, inasmuch as a man who sins a second time sins more grievously than when he first sinned. Hence it may be laid down that remitted sins do not return absolutely, but relatively only, inasmuch as they are virtually contained in subsequent sin.

CCX. The remission of sins in penitence being accomplished by the infusion of grace, there flow from grace all gratuitous virtues, even as from the essence of the soul flow all the powers of the soul.

CCXI. Since the motion of free will, which, in the justification of the ungodly, is the last disposition to grace, is sometimes more intense, and sometimes more remiss in penitence than before; and since, according to this intensity or remissness, is the proportion of grace greater or less, it follows that the penitent may rise again greater, equal, or less, in grace and virtue than when he fell.

CCXII. By penitence a man may return to his principal dignity, which by sinning he has lost, to the dignity that is of being a son of God. But innocence once lost can never be regained, any more than can virginity. It is forbidden to restore to a sinner his ecclesiastical dignity—1. Who is not penitent; 2. Or who has done his penance negligently; 3. Who has forfeited it by irregularity; or, 4. To avoid occasion of scandal.

CCXIII. Works done in charity are said to be mortified or become dead by mortal sin, inasmuch as their effect, the attainment of eternal life, is thereby retarded or hindered; but reviving by penitence, they regain the power of producing their effect. But works originally dead—that is, works not done in charity, can never be quickened by repentance, having never had within them a principle of life.

CCXIV. The parts of penitence are—1. *Contrition*, whereby the sinner desires to recompense God. 2. *Confession*, whereby for the remission of his guilt he subjects himself to the judgment of the priest in the place of God. 3. And *Satisfaction*, whereby he satisfies God according to the judgment of God's minister. In order to perfect penitence there is required the contrition of the heart, the confession of the mouth, and the satisfaction of the deed.

CCXV. Penance, as it is a virtue, is divided into—1. Penance before baptism, which is not a sacrament, but an act of virtue disposing to the sacrament of baptism. 2. Penance from mortal sins, which is sacramental; and 3. Penance from venial sins, which are remitted as shewn above, by some fervent act of charity.

CCXVI. Contrition may be defined to be, A sorrow for sin, with a purpose of confession and satisfaction.

CCXVII. Since there is not found in the pains of sin any hardness of the will, of which hardness contrition signifies the diminution, there cannot be contrition save concerning the *guilt* of sin. There may be sorrow for the pains of sin, but not contrition.

CCXVIII. Contrition as a sorrow, diminishing in some measure the hardness of the will contracted from sin, does not properly concern original sin, which has not been induced by our will, but rather contracted by the origin of our corrupted nature. There may be a certain displeasure or sorrow concerning it, but not contrition.

CCXIX. There must be contrition for all and every actual sin. Contrition, as a part of penitence, regards the past, and so one does not sorrow for, but, as a part of prudence, guards against future sin. There may be sorrow, but not contrition for another's sin.

CCXX. Oblivion is twofold, partial and total—a matter may be altogether forgotten, as there may be a general, although not a special, recollection of it. When a sin has entirely passed from the memory, general contrition is sufficient, as there can, of course, be no special contrition. But should it be recalled to the memory, special contrition becomes a duty. When, after due diligence, it is found that the special circumstances of a mortal sin have passed from the memory, there must be, 1. Contrition corresponding to the remembrance of the sin; 2. Contrition for the negligence which has permitted it to escape.

CCXXI. Contrition, properly and essentially so called, that sorrow namely, which exists in the will whereby one sorrows for his sins as contrary to his Last End, is rightly said to be the greatest of all sorrows. But not so that sorrow caused in the sensitive part of man's nature either as an effect of the first, Contrition proper, or excited therein by the penitent himself. These sorrows of the sensitive part of man's nature are much more easily caused through his body than through his soul. This sorrow may be excessive, the former cannot be. The sorrow ought to be infinite for sins which are infinite, because they offend an Infinite God.

CCXXII. Since by past sin the course of our life toward God is retarded and hindered, a man ought during the whole term of his life here on earth to sorrow and be contrite for his past sins.

CCXXIII. In Contrition three things are to be considered. 1. Its *genus*, which is sorrow. 2. Its *form*, which is an act of virtue informed by grace. 3. Its *efficacy*, which is a meritorious and sacramental, and in a measure satisfactory act. But the souls which, after this life, are in their Fatherland, lack sorrow by reason of their plenitude of joy. 2. Those in hell have sorrow, but not informed by grace. 3. Those in purgatory have a sorrow for sin, informed by grace but not meritorious, because they are not in a state of meriting. In this life all these three conditions are found, but after this life, one or other is wanting in purgatory, in heaven, or in hell, and so after this life there can be no contrition.

CCXXIV. Contrition, as it is an act of virtue dispositively, but as it is part of a sacrament, effectively and instrumentally causes the remission of sins. Contrition, whether in regard of charity, or in regard of sensible sorrow, may be so great as to suffice to the full destruction of pain and guilt. Sorrow, however little, so that it suffice to the idea of Contrition, destroys all guilt.

CCXXV. The Passion of Christ, apart from the virtue of which neither original nor actual sin is remitted, operates in us by our reception of the Sacraments, which derive their efficacy therefrom. And so without the reception of the Sacraments, either actual or desired, there can be no remission. Now, there are two Sacraments ordained to take away guilt, baptism and penance. As the one is necessary, so also is the other. Since Penance cannot be administered to any one for a remedy, unless the sin be known, for what is unknown cannot be cured, Sacramental Confession is of necessity to salvation for those who have fallen into actual mortal sin.

As in secular Courts the judge and the accused are never one and the same person; so in the tribunal of penance the sinner who is the accused ought not to be his own judge. He ought to be judged by another, and so must needs confess to him.

CCXXVI. Since the Sacraments are not of the Natural Law but of the Divine Law, as belonging to faith which transcends Natural reason, it follows that Sacramental Confession is not of the Natural but of the Divine Law.

CCXXVII. Although, of divine law, sinners only are bound to confess, yet of positive law, that is by appointment of the Church, published in the Lateran Council, under Innocent III., all Christ's faithful, of both sexes, who have come to the years of discretion, are bound to confess their sins at least once a-year; or, if free from mortal sin, to declare their freedom to a priest. But ordinarily, although not sacramentally necessary, those who have no mortal sins, confess their venial sins.

CCXXVIII. In confession, the penitent lays bare his conscience to his priest, and so the mouth must accuse only what the conscience contains. Whosoever says that he has committed a sin which he has not, lies. When he is in doubt whether a sin he has committed be mortal, he is bound to confess it, and commit the judgment thereof to the priest.

CCXXIX. Although all men are bound immediately to sorrow, and be contrite for their sins, with a purpose of confession and satisfaction—and confession may not be delayed without peril—yet it is not of necessity to salvation that one immediately confess one's sins, unless one is bound to do something which he may not do after mortal sin without having confessed it, as a priest to celebrate, or a layman to receive the Holy Eucharist at Easter.

CCXXX. It does not belong to the ministry of the Church to propose new articles of faith, nor to abolish those already received; so neither does it belong to them to institute new Sacraments, nor to dispense with those already ordained. And so, as no Ecclesiastical authority can dispense with the necessity of Baptism to salvation, neither can any dispense with the necessity of

Confession, which, as an integral part of the Sacrament of Penance, is of Divine law. The stated season of Confession, which is matter of positive and ecclesiastical law, may be dispensed by the competent authority.

CCXXXI. S. Augustine defines Confession to be that whereby the hidden disease is laid bare with the hope of pardon. S. Gregory calls it the rupture of the wound. In the act of Confession there is to be considered, 1. its substance or genus, which is a manifestation; 2. its matter, which is sin; 3. to whom it is made, namely, to a priest; 4. its cause, to wit, hope of pardon; 5. its effects, and they are, absolution from part of the pain, and an obligation to undergo the remainder. Confession wherein the heart and mouth agree is an act of virtue and meritorious; as the Master of the Sentences says, It opens heaven.

CCXXXII. Christ signified Confession in sending the lepers whom He had healed to the Jewish priests: Go shew yourselves to the priest. And, in the command to His disciples concerning Lazarus, whom He had raised from the dead, Loose him, and let him go.

CCXXXIII. The grace which is given in the Sacraments descends from the Head to the members, and therefore he alone is minister of the Sacraments in which grace is given, who has ministry over the True Body of Christ: and this belongs to a priest only who can consecrate the Eucharist. Since, therefore, there is grace conferred in the Sacrament of Penance, a priest only is the proper minister thereof. In extreme necessity, and where a priest cannot be had, Confession may be made to a laic, and this Confession will be in a manner Sacramental, as containing the penitent's part, although lacking the priest's part, namely, absolution, which perfects the Sacrament. But he who confesses to a laic will not be admitted to reception of the Holy Eucharist; and he is bound, in case of opportunity, to repeat his Confession to a priest. As venial sins separate a man neither from God, nor from the Sacraments of the Church, Confession of them to a priest is not necessary, as the penitent needs neither new grace, nor reconciliation with the Church. Confession to a laic being a sacramental, although not a perfect sacrament, they are remitted thereby, as by beating the breast, by sprinkling of Blessed Water, or any other like act proceeding from charity.

CCXXXIV. The Minister of this Sacrament must have not only power of Order, but power of *jurisdiction*, and so confession is not to be made save to one's own parish priest, without licence, either from him, or from the Bishop, or other superior, or competent authority: except in peril of death, when the penitent may be absolved by any priest whomsoever, not only from all his sins, but from all excommunications whatsoever, by whomsoever imposed.

CCXXXV. Punishment is exacted after remission of guilt—1, in order to pay a debt; 2, in order to afford a remedy. 1. In the first case the pain is to be taxed according to the measure of the fault. 2. In the second, regard is to be had to the condition of the person.

CCXXXVI. Confession, as it is a part of the Sacrament of Penance, may sometimes be made by one who is not contrite, and who is without charity; but as it is an act of virtue it cannot properly be in any one without charity, which is the principle of merit in every act of virtue. Confession without contrition is invalid, but becomes valid by subsequent contrition. This fact is to be confessed, but the confession itself is not to be iterated.

CCXXXVII. A physician must not only know the one disease against which he is to prescribe a remedy, but be familiar with the general habit of his patient, because not only is one disease aggravated by the presence of another, but the medicine which is useful for the one may become hurtful by reason of the other. The case is precisely similar in sins, the diseases of the soul; and so it is of necessity to confession that a man confess all the sins which he has in his memory. If he do not, it is not confession, but a pretence of confession.

CCXXXVIII. Confession, as it is an act of virtue, may be made in any way; but as it is a part of the Sacrament of Penance, it has a determinate act as the other Sacraments have determinate matter, and can be made only by one's own mouth, and not by the mouth of another, or in writing, unless the penitent be dumb, or a foreigner, when writing, signs or an interpreter may be employed.

CCXXXIX. Of the sixteen conditions of confession contained in the following verses, some are of precept and some of counsel, that is, some are of necessity and some are advisable. Some regard Confession as it is an act of virtue, and some as it is a part of the Sacrament of Penance:

> Sit simplex, humilis confessio, pura, fidelis,
> Atque frequens, nuda et discreta, libens verecunda,
> Integra, secreta, lachrymabilis, accelerata,
> Fortis, et accusans, et sit parere parata.

i. Confession, as it is an act of virtue, must be—1, *discreta*, for prudence is required in the act of every virtue; 2, *libens*, for an act of virtue must be voluntary; 3, *pura*, there must be a right intention; 4, *fortis*, the truth must not be concealed from shame; 5, *verecunda*, there must be no pride or glorying in the sins confessed; 6, *lachrymabilis*, but on the contrary, sorrow for having committed them; 7, *humilis*, there must be self-abjection and acknowledgment of infirmity; 8, *fidelis*, it must be entirely true; 9, *nuda*, and neither obscured by hard words; 10, *simplex*, nor hidden by a multitude of them; 11, *integra*, but entire, full and complete. ii. As it is a part of the Sacrament of Penance it must be: 12, *accusans*, as regards the penitent; 13, *parere parata*, as regards the priest: 14, *secreta*, as regards the matters revealed. iii. It is not indeed of absolute necessity, but very advisable, that it be: 15, *frequens*; and 16, *accelerata*, made as soon as possible after the commission of any mortal sin.

CCXL. Confession accompanied by contrition, satisfaction and absolution, sets free the penitent from the death of sin, from the eternal pains as well as from the guilt of sin, and also, according to his dispositions, diminishes the temporal pains. It opens to him Paradise, and affords him a hope of salvation.

CCXLI. In the sacraments the outward and visible is a sign of the inward and invisible. The outward subjection of one's self to the priest in confession is a sign of the inward subjection of one's self to God. As God always covers the sins of those who subject themselves to Him by repentance, so ought His priest always to conceal the sins of those who subject themselves to him by confession. Besides the sacramental necessity of this concealment, it is useful in other ways, for by reason of it men are induced to confess, and to confess more freely and unreservedly than they would otherwise do. No one can be either compelled or licensed to reveal confessions. If a question be put, and an answer demanded under pain of excommunication, he may say that he knows nothing, for he knows nothing as man, only as God; and, moreover, he will not incur excommunication, because he is not subject to his superior, save as he is a man—and the matter of confession he knows not as man, but as God. A prelate hears confessions and applies remedies, not as he is a prelate, but as he is a priest, and so deals with sins, not as affecting his own interests or the interests of his subjects, but as affecting the soul of his penitent. Although the Seal of Confession, properly and directly, extends to those things only which are matter of Sacramental Confession, yet indirectly, and to avoid scandal, it extends to cognate subjects. Although, properly, the Seal of Confession pertains only to the priest, yet, as a laic hearing a confession of necessity, shares somewhat of the act of the Keys, so he also shares somewhat of the Seal of Confession, and is held bound to conceal what has been revealed to him. The Penitent may cause the Priest to know what he knows as God—as man also, and give him leave to reveal it. But the greatest care must be taken to avoid scandal, and prevent a suspicion that the Seal has been broken. And the like care must be observed with regard to what he has learned otherwise than by Confession, whether before or after. The general rule in every case being that there are two reasons wherefore the priest is held bound to conceal sin. 1. First and principally, because this concealment is of the essence of the Sacrament, inasmuch as what he knows he knows as God, whose place he occupies; 2. and secondly, to avoid scandal.

CCXLII. Satisfaction is said to be not only materially an act of virtue, as any act may be called which does not imply implicit malice or defect of due circumstance; but also formally, as containing in its name the implicit form and idea of virtue.

Like every act of virtue it is meritorious, and to be meritorious it must be gratuitous. Doubtless satisfaction has regard to debt, but he who satisfies voluntarily, by that voluntariness gives it *ex parte* of him the idea of gratuity, and so he makes of necessity a virtue. If the will consent to the necessity, the idea of merit is not thereby taken away.

According to the Philosopher, Ethics, v. 3, the mean of justice is taken according to the adequation of one thing to another in a certain proportion, and so, since the very name of satisfaction imports such an adequation, Satisfaction is formally an act of justice.

CCXLIII. Since, in respect of past guilt, satisfaction is a recompensation of the injury done thereby, S. Anselm in his book, Cur Deus Homo, i. 11, defines it to be a payment to God of the honour which is His due. In respect of preservation from future guilt, S. Augustine defines it to be—to cut out the causes of sin, and to refuse an entrance to its suggestions.

CCXLIV. Man is the debtor of God—1, by reason of benefits received; 2, by reason of sins committed. As thanksgiving or *latria* is to the one, so is satisfaction to the other. If satisfaction imports equality of quantity, man cannot satisfy God; but if it signifies equality of proportion, he may.

CCXLV. As the offence had a certain infinity from the infinity of the Divine Majesty, so has also the satisfaction a certain infinity from the infinity of the Divine Mercy; it being informed by grace whereby what man can do is rendered acceptable.

CCXLVI. Satisfactory pain is ordained for two ends—1, for payment of debt; 2, as a remedy for the avoidance of future sin. The satisfaction of one person may profit another so far as the first, but not so far as the second is concerned, unless it be *per accidens*, the good works of the one meriting for the other an increase of grace, the most efficacious remedy against sin.

CCXLVII. Since by satisfaction there is taken away the offence of the previous sin, and the taking away of the offence is the restoration of the Divine friendship, which restoration is hindered by the continued presence of any sin whatsoever, it follows that a man cannot satisfy for one sin and retain another. In other words, satisfaction is a medicine which cures past and preserves from future sins. Both preservation and cure are the result of grace, which cannot co-exist in the soul with sin. And so a man cannot satisfy for one sin without satisfying for another.

CCXLVIII. Since works done apart from charity are not acceptable to God, no man existing out of charity with God can satisfy for sins, the guilt and eternal pain of which have been previously remitted by contrition. Nor can these dead works be quickened, that is, be made satisfactory and meritorious of eternal life, by subsequent charity. Works originally living become deadened by intervening sin, but revive by subsequent charity. Not so works originally dead; in them has never existed life to be revived.

L

CCXLIX. Merit is properly that action whereby it is effected that to him who acts there is a *just* reward to be given. But justice is two-fold. In one way and properly, it has regard to that which is due *ex parte* of the recipient. In another way, and by way of similitude, it has regard to that which is due *ex parte* of the giver; for it may become the giver to give something which is not due to the receiver, and which he cannot claim of right. And so justice is said to be that which becomes the Divine Goodness; as S. Anselm says, God is just when He spares sinners, because it becomes Him. According to this distinction merit is two-fold. In one way that act by which it is effected that he who acts has himself a right to receive, and this is called *meritum condigni*. In another way, that by which it is effected that there lies on the giver a debt of giving, by reason of its becomingness; and this is called *meritum congrui*. Now, since in all those things which are given of grace, the first reason of giving is love, it is impossible that any one can properly cause anything to be due to himself who is out of the friendship of God. Therefore, since all things, both temporal and eternal, are given to us of the Divine liberality, no man can acquire a right or claim to receive any of those things unless by charity towards God, and so works done apart from charity are not meritorious *ex condigno* of any benefit of God, whether temporal or eternal. But because it becomes the Divine goodness to add perfection wherever it finds disposition, so one may be said to merit some good, by works done apart from charity, *ex congruo*. And according to this these works avail towards a threefold good. 1. The attainment of temporal good things. 2. Disposition to grace. 3. Accustoming to good works. But since this merit is not merit properly so called, we ought rather to say that works of this sort are not meritorious of any good than to say that they are.

CCL. Whether as regards recompensation of the past, or remedy for the future, satisfactory works must be good, to the honour of God, and penal. The sufferings of this present life, inflicted by God, may be appropriated by the penitent by a patient endurance, and so become voluntary, satisfactory, and meritorious. Apart from a loving patience, which makes a virtue out of necessity, they have the character of vengeance rather than of satisfaction.

CCLI. The three satisfactory works are—1, Prayer; 2, Fasting; and 3, Almsgiving. ii. Satisfactory works take from ourselves to give to God. All that we may take from to give, is what we are and what we have. What we are is our body and soul; what we have is our substance. 1, We take from our body by fasting; 2, from our soul by prayer; 3, from our substance by almsgiving. iii. Fasting is ordained against the lust of the flesh; 2, almsgiving against the lust of the eye; 3, and prayer against the pride of life. iv. All our sins are against—1, God; 2, our neighbour; 3, ourselves. Against these are ordained—1, Prayer; 2, Almsgiving; 3, Fasting. v. They correspond, moreover, to the three vows of religion: 1, Fasting—Chastity; 2, Almsgiving—Poverty; 3, Prayer—Obedience. vi. 1, Fasting includes whatever tends to the affliction of our bodies; 2, Almsgiving, whatever tends to the welfare of our neighbour; 3, Prayer, whatever tends to God's greater honour and glory.

CCLII. Since the innocent in a state of innocence have committed no sin, there cannot be in them an act of penitence, because there is not in them sin, which is the matter of penitence. But they may sin, and so there will be in them a habit of penitence, which along with all other virtues has been infused into them when they received grace. As he who has never been bodily infirm may yet be said to be capable of healing, because he may hereafter be infirm and require it; so in like manner with him who has never been spiritually infirm. Christ could not sin, and so the matter of penitence could not pertain to Him either in possibility, in habit, or in act.

CCLIII. Since the cardinal virtues will remain in fatherland, and penitence is part of the cardinal virtue of justice, the saints in glory will have it; not the same act as now, however, but another, namely, to give thanks to God for His mercy in relieving them from their sins.

CCLIV. Penitence, as it is a passion, that is, a grief, a sorrow for evil committed, existing in the *Concupiscible*, belongs to evil angels; but not penitence, as it is a virtue having a purpose of amendment and an intention of expiation. Neither as a passion nor as a virtue does it belong to the good angels, who neither have nor could have committed remissible sin.

CCLV. Among things corporal that instrument is called a key wherewith a door is opened. Now the gate of heaven is shut against us by sin, by reason both of its stain and of its *reatus pœnæ*, and so the power whereby that obstacle is removed is called a key.

This power exists in the Divine Trinity by *authority*. They are therefore said to have the *key of authority*.

It exists in the Man Christ by the merits of his Passion, which, as removing the obstacle, are said to open the gate of heaven. He is, therefore, said to have the *keys of excellency*. From the Side of Christ sleeping on the cross flowed the Sacraments, by means of which the Church has been built up. In those Sacraments the efficacy of the Passion remains and resides. And so, on the ministers of the Church, as the dispensers of the Sacraments which remove the obstacle, has been conferred by Christ, in virtue of the merits of His Passion, the power of opening and shutting the gates of the kingdom of heaven. They are therefore said to have the *keys of ministry*.

CCLVI. In the Revelation S. John looked, and behold, a door was opened in heaven. This door He opened who says of Himself, I am the door. He opened it to *whole human nature* by removing the impediment common to whole human nature. But in order to open it to the *individual*, by removing the impediments special to the individual, there are yet required the Sacraments and keys of the Church.

CCLVII. The Church is said to have the Keys of Heaven, but is not said to have the Keys of Hell; and for this reason: The key of hell, whereby it is opened and shut, is the power of conferring grace. By grace hell is opened to a man to escape from sin, which is the gate of hell. By grace sustaining a man, hell is shut to him, lest he fall again through sin thereinto. But the power of conferring grace belongs to God alone, and so He has retained for Himself alone the Key of Hell.

The Key of the Kingdom, moreover, is a power also of remitting the *reatus* of temporal punishment, which remains and hinders an entrance to the Kingdom. And so the Key of the Kingdom may be given to man rather than the Key of Hell. For they are not one and the same; one who has been rescued from hell by remission of the eternal punishment is not immediately admitted into Heaven, by reason of the *reatus* of temporal punishment which remains.

In one sense the two keys are identical, and in this sense, inasmuch as the greater includes the less, the Church is said to have the Key of Heaven as the greater of the two.

CCLVIII. The use of the Key requiring previous fitness on the part of the recipient, in respect of him the Key is said to be double. One is called the *science of discerning*, as pertaining to a judgment of the fitness of him who is to be absolved. The other is called the *power of judging*, as pertaining to the absolution itself.

The first may exist in a learned laic; the second only in a priest, in whom, however, it may exist unaccompanied by the first—just as in the case of secular judges, and learned jurists not judges. A judge may be ignorant of the law, yet have the power of judging; while a jurist, not a judge, may be learned in the law, and so have knowledge to discern, without the power of putting that knowledge into force.

Both the knowledge and the power are in either case requisite, in order to judging well.

CCLIX. God alone *per se* remits *guilt*, the priest *ministerialiter*, as His animate instrument in like manner as in baptism, the washing with water in the Name of the Trinity with intention to baptize acts as His inanimate instrument.

CCLX. The whole *reatus* of eternal punishment is remitted along with the guilt, and a part, but not the whole, of the temporal punishment. There is also conferred increase of grace.

CCLXI. The operation of the priest in the use of the Keys is conformed to the operation of God, whose minister he is. Now, God operates on both guilt and punishment *(culpa* and *pœna)*; on guilt *directly*, by loosing therefrom; *indirectly*, by binding, inasmuch as He is said to harden, when He does not vouchsafe grace. On the punishment He operates directly in both cases, whether He remit it or inflict it. Similarly also the priest operates in order to the remission of the *guilt*, as in manner foresaid, not *per se*, but *ministerialiter*, but in respect of it, he is not said to bind save as, in not absolving, he leaves bound, and declares bound. But with regard to the temporal punishment, he has power both of binding and loosing, for he looses from the punishment which he remits; he binds to the punishment which remains, and this not only by leaving and declaring bound, but by binding.

CCLXII. Were there no other reason, the Passion of Christ would oblige men to pain in some measure, inasmuch as they must be conformed thereto.

Hence a baptized child, freed by its baptism from all trace of sin, whether of *culpa*, *macula*, or *reatus*, and having never deserved temporal punishment by actual sin, must yet, inasmuch as it is conformed to Christ, suffer, die, and be buried with and in Him, in order that with and in Him it may rise again to the Life Eternal a glorified member of His glorious Body.

CCLXIII. As the priest operates in the use of the Keys as the minister and instrument of God, and as no instrument is efficacious to act—save as it is moved by the principal agent—so if a priest presume to exercise his power according to his own will, and otherwise than as according to the ordinance of God, his principal agent, it will fail of its effect.

Satisfactory punishments are to be inflicted by way of medicine. And just as in the material world, the medicines determined by the medical art will not apply in all cases, but must be varied according to the judgment of the physician, following not the dictates of his own will, but the conclusions of medical science, so in the spiritual world, the satisfactory punishments determined in the Canons will not apply in all cases, but must be varied according to the judgment of the priest, regulated by divine instinct.

As, therefore, the physician acts with prudence when he sometimes does not give that medicine which is most efficacious for the cure of the disease, to avoid greater evils likely to arise from debility of nature; so the priest, moved by a divine instinct, does not always enjoin the full penalty due to any one sin, lest peradventure in his infirmity, the sinner despair at the magnitude of his punishment, and wholly cease from his repentance.

CCLXIV. Since the power of the priests under the law did not extend to Heavenly things, but only to the figures of Heavenly things, they did not possess the Keys, but only figures foreshadowing the Keys.

The Keys are ordained in order to the opening the Kingdom of Heaven, but before the Passion of Christ, the gate of Heaven was not opened to believers.

The Sacraments of the Old Law neither contained nor conferred grace. But an entrance to the Heavenly Kingdom cannot be opened save by grace, and so neither were these sacraments efficacious thereunto; nor could the priests, their ministers, be said to have the Keys of the Kingdom. They had the Keys, not of Heaven, but of the figure of Heaven, the earthly tabernacle;

and they had the power of discerning and judging, and of purging, not from spiritual guilt, but from legal irregularities, by means of legal sacraments.

CCLXV. Christ had the power of the Keys as He was God by *authority*, as He was man by *merit*. In the one case He acts as principal agent, in the other ministerially, but after a manner higher than that of others His ministers, and so He is said to have the Key of excellency.

He hath the Key of David; He openeth and no man shutteth, and shutteth and no man openeth.

CCLXVI. The *Key of Order*, which has immediate reference to the Kingdom of Heaven, as, by remission of sins, removing obstacles to entrance thereon, pertains to priests alone. The *Key of Jurisdiction*, which has immediate reference, not to heaven, but to the passage to Heaven, the Church militant here on earth, from which one is excluded, and to which one is readmitted respectively by excommunication and loosing the bonds thereof—pertains not only to priests, but to archdeacons, and others having power of excommunication.

This, however, is not properly called the Key of Heaven, but is only somewhat dispositive thereto.

Ostiarii have the key of the custody of those things which are contained in the material temple, and have a judicial power of excluding from and admitting to that temple, not indeed as by their own authority judging who are worthy and who unworthy, but as carrying into execution the judgment of the priests.

Kings have no power in spiritual matters, and so do not receive the key of the kingdom of heaven. They have power only in things temporal, and this only as from God. Neither are they by their anointing consecrated to any sacred order, but the excellency of their power derived from Christ is thereby signified, as reigning under Christ over Christian people.

The Key of order pertains to every individual priest; but power of jurisdiction may be vested in an individual, or in a congregation of individuals, as in a Bishop or in a Chapter.

Woman is, according to the Apostle, in a state of subjection, and so cannot have any spiritual jurisdiction. Hence a woman has neither the Key of order nor the Key of jurisdiction. But to certain women, as to abbesses, is committed a power of correction of those women subjected to their rule, by reason of the perils attendant on the cohabitation of men with women in the same house.

CLXVII. Since *pure man* can never be more than an instrumental agent, however much grace he may have, he cannot attain to the power and use of the Keys without the reception of sacerdotal order, whereby he becomes a minister or instrumental agent of Christ, the principal agent.

CLXVIII. A wicked priest, although he be deprived of grace, is yet in no way thereby deprived of the use of the Keys, for, as participation of the form does not make the instrument, so neither does subtraction of such form take away the use of the instrument.

The minister's iniquity cannot take away the Lord's liberality.

No man knows of another whether or not he be in a state of salvation. If, therefore, no priest could use the Keys and absolve, unless he were in a state of grace, no man would know whether or not he was absolved!

The gift of the Holy Ghost was, and is, given in ordination in order to the use of the Keys, according to the text, Receive ye the Holy Ghost: Whosesoever sins ye remit, they are remitted unto them, and whosesoever sins ye retain, they are retained; but not as of such necessity as that without it this power could not be possessed and exercised; for, although without it there would be an incongruity on the part of the user, yet he who subjected himself to the Keys would obtain this effect.

An earthly king may be deceived and defrauded of his treasures, and so he commits not the dispensation of them to his enemy: but the King of Heaven, who knows how to bring good out of evil, and by evil men to do many good deeds, and to turn even the wrath of man to His praise, cannot be deceived or defrauded of the treasures of His grace, the dispensation of which He sometimes commits to wicked ministers.

CCLXIX. Schismatick, heretick, excommunicated, suspended and degraded priests do indeed retain and possess the power of the Keys as to *its essence*, but they are hindered from *its use* by want of matter—that is, by want of subjects. As by the ordaining of the Church, one man is subjected to another who is set over him, so by the Prelates of the Church this order may be altered or disannulled: and thus a priest possessing the essential power of the Keys, in virtue of his indelible power of order, may be hindered from its actual exercise, from having, by the withdrawal of his power of jurisdiction, no subjects or matter on which to exercise it.

CCLXX. A prelate, who has an indistinct, that is, an undefined power over all, can use the power of the keys upon all; but those who have received from him distinct, that is, defined and limited powers, can use the keys on those only who have been committed to them, save only in the last necessity, when the Sacraments are to be denied to no man, for necessity has no law.

CCLXXI. The Lord gave to all the Apostles *communiter* the power of remitting sins, as a power of order: to Peter *singulariter*, as a power also of jurisdiction.

CCLXXII. As a material key cannot open save its own lock, so cannot an active virtue operate save on its own matter. Hence no priest can loose or bind save those set under him, and placed by authority within his jurisdiction.

CCLXXIII. The priests of the Old Law could use their power of discerning in the case of leprosy indifferently with regard to all; but then the people of Israel was one people, and had only one temple, and so there was no necessity that their priests should have distinct and defined jurisdictions, as now in the Church, within which congregate diverse peoples and nations.

As a temporal judge may not judge whom he will, so, in like manner, a spiritual judge may not judge whom he will, but those only committed to his jurisdiction.

CCLXXIV. Power of order *per se* extends to the remission of all sins, but as in order to the use of this power there is required jurisdiction, which descends from superiors to inferiors, so a superior may reserve to himself certain sins, the judgment of which he does not commit to his inferiors: otherwise a simple priest having jurisdiction could absolve from all sins whatsoever.

There are five cases in which a simple priest must remit the penitent to his superior—1. when a solemn penance is to be imposed, because its proper minister is the Bishop; 2. persons excommunicate by a superior, whom a simple priest cannot absolve; 3. a case of irregularity, which requires the superior's dispensation in order to its remission; 4. incendiaries; 5. when it is the custom in any diocese, for a terror to evil-doers, to reserve enormous crimes to the Bishop. Custom, in such cases, gives power or takes it away.

CCLXXV. A priest ought not to hear the confession of a woman with whom he has sinned, concerning that sin, but ought to send her to another; neither ought she to confess to him, but to ask his leave to go to another, or have recourse to his superior, if he deny that leave. This, however, of congruity only, to avoid peril and increase shame, not of sacramental necessity, for if the criminous priest absolve her, she is absolved.

CCLXXVI. Penance liberates from all defects of guilt, but not from all defects of punishment. For instance, there remains after penance done for homicide an irregularity; and so, while a simple priest can absolve a penitent from the guilt of his sin, he must send him to his superiors for the removal of his irregularity.

In excommunication, however, absolution from it ought to precede absolution from sin, because so long as one is excommunicate, one cannot receive any sacrament of the Church.

CCLXXVII. Since a superior prelate cannot use the keys on himself —for no man can be at once superior and subject, judge and judged—and since he who limits the power of his inferior can also extend it as he wills, an inferior may use the keys on his superior, if that superior subject himself *pro tempore* to his power, which power would be universal were it not limited.

CCLXXVIII. He who is placed by Baptism in the Church, is—1, enrolled in the Company of the Faithful, and 2, has a right to participation of the Sacraments. The second presupposes the first, because in the participation of the Sacraments the faithful have fellowship one with another. And so one may be placed outside the Church in two ways. In one way, by being separated only from participation of the Sacraments. This is the *Lesser Excommunication*. In another way, by being excluded from both the participation of the Sacraments and the fellowship of the faithful. This is the *Greater Excommunication*. There cannot be a third way: there cannot be exclusion from the communion of the faithful, and not from participation of the Sacraments, for the reason foresaid, that the faithful communicate with each other in and through the Sacraments.

The communications of the faithful are twofold; in spiritual matters, as mutual prayers and assemblies for the reception of things sacred: and secondly, in lawful corporal acts. The communications debarred from are contained in the verses:—

> Si pro delictis anathema quis efficiatur :
> Os, orare, vale, communio, mensa negatur.

Os, that no kiss be given: *orare*, that no man unite in common prayer with the excommunicate: *vale*, nor salute him by the way: *communio*, nor have fellowship with him in sacraments: *mensa*, nay, with such an one no, not to eat.

CCLXXIX. Prayers are made by the Church for those beyond her pale, as for the unbelieving and the excommunicate, but they do not receive the fruit of these prayers unless and until they be converted to the faith, and restored to the unity of the faithful. They are prayed for by the Church, not as members, but that there may be given them the spirit of penitence, and grace to become living members of the One Body.

CCLXXX. The Church is the vicegerent of God on the earth; occupying as such the place of God, her judgment ought to be conformed to the judgment of God. Now, God punishes sinners in manifold ways, in order to draw them to good. Sometimes He corrects them with stripes. At other times He leaves man to himself, and withdraws from him His aid, in order that he may know by experience his own infirmity, and return in humility to his God, from whom, in his pride, he had gone far away. Both of these Divine methods the Church imitates in her sentence of excommunication. She corrects with stripes in separating the sinner from the fellowship of the faithful. She withdraws her aids, in separating him from prayers and sacraments.

CCLXXXI. Separation from the prayers of the Church works a threefold loss, corresponding to the threefold gain which participation in them operates —1. They avail to the increase of grace in those who have it, and to merit grace for those who have it not. 2. They avail to the preservation of virtue. 3. They avail to defence from the enemy. In this sense is to be understood what the Master of the Sentences says—1, that by excommunication the grace of God is withdrawn. 2, That His protection also is withheld—not that the excommunicated are altogether excluded from the providence of God, but from that protection wherewith, in a more special manner. He surrounds the children of the Church. 3, That the Devil has greater power, both corporal and spiritual, over the excommunicated than over others.

CCLXXXII. S. Paul directs the Corinthians to deliver their incestuous brother unto Satan, for the destruction of the flesh, that the spirit might be saved in the day of the Lord Jesus. And this was a custom in the Primitive Church. The excommunicated person was not, as despaired of, given over to the enemy for damnation, but for correction, seeing it was in the power of the Church at her will to deliver him out of the enemy's hand.

Jesus said to his disciples: If (a man) neglect to hear the Church, let him be unto thee as an heathen man and a publican.

CCLXXXIII. Since by mortal sin a man is rendered unworthy of the kingdom, whosoever, in inflicting on another a temporal loss, sins mortally, may be excommunicated therefor.

But seeing excommunication is the most grievous of all punishments, and it is a maxim in medicine to begin with the lighter before proceeding to the more severe remedies—excommunication ought not to be inflicted even for mortal sin, unless the sinner be contumacious, either by not coming to judgment, or departing before its termination without licence, or by not submitting to the sentence. Having been admonished, and scorning to obey, he will thereupon be pronounced contumacious and excommunicated—there being nothing farther that the judge can do with him.

CCLXXXIV. An excommunication may be called unjust in two ways. In one way, *ex parte* of him who excommunicates, as when one excommunicates from anger or hatred. In this case the excommunication, if in itself just, will nevertheless have its effect, although he who excommunicates sins, for the one justly suffers, although the other unjustly acts. 2. An excommunication may be unjust *ex parte* of the excommunication itself, either because the cause of excommunication was undue, or because sentence has been pronounced without regular process of law, and thus if there be such error on the part of the sentence as to make it to be no sentence, the excommunication has no effect, because it is, in point of fact, not an excommunication. But if the error is not such as to annul the sentence, it has its effect, and the excommunicated ought humbly to obey it (and it will be to him for merit), or to seek absolution from the excommunicator, or to have recourse to a superior judge. But if he treat the excommunication with contempt, he thereby sins mortally.

But it sometimes happens that there is due cause *ex parte* of him who excommunicates, and not due cause *ex parte* of the excommunicated, as when one is excommunicated for a crime falsely alleged but judicially proved against him. In this case, if the excommunicated humbly bear it, the merit of his humility will recompense the loss of his excommunication.

CCLXXXV. Only bishops and the greater prelates can excommunicate, as having jurisdiction *in foro judiciali*, to which excommunication, as separating a man from the communion of the faithful, appertains.

Excommunication, being a very perilous punishment, and so to be inflicted only with the greatest moderation, parish priests cannot excommunicate unless the power has been committed to them, or in certain cases, as theft, rapine, or the like, in which it has been by the law conceded to them.

As excommunication is not *directly* concerned with grace, but *indirectly*, as depriving men of the suffrages of the church, which dispose to, and preserve in grace, so persons who are not priests may excommunicate if they have jurisdiction *in foro contentioso*, as in the case of archdeacons, legates, &c.

Since an excommunicated person is separated from the communion of the faithful, and deprived of the use of jurisdiction, and a suspended person cannot perform those acts which require jurisdiction, neither can excommunicate.

As he who is himself corporeally bound cannot bind another, so he who is himself spiritually bound by the bond of excommunication cannot bind another.

As no man can have jurisdiction over himself, or his superior, or his equal, so no man can excommunicate himself, or his superior, or his equal— excommunication being an act of jurisdiction.

CCLXXXVI. No one ought to be excommunicated save for mortal sin; but sin consists in an act, and an act, generally speaking, pertains not to a community, but to the individual members thereof who consent thereto. And so they, and not the community, ought to be excommunicated.

The Church ought to imitate the judgment of God, who does not condemn the just with the unjust, and not excommunicate communities, lest peradventure with the tares the wheat also should be rooted up.

Suspension is not so great a punishment as excommunication, because the suspended are not defrauded of the suffrages of the Church, as are the excommunicate; and so sometimes a whole kingdom is placed under an interdict *a divinis*, for the sin of its king.

CCLXXXVII. He who has been excommunicated by one excommunication, may be again excommunicated, either by iteration of the same excommunication, to his greater confusion, that so he may resile from his sin, or by a fresh excommunication for a fresh cause.

There may be as many principal excommunications as there are due causes; and each succeeding excommunication removes the excommunicated person farther from the suffrages of the Church; for although deprivation does not admit the ideas of more and less, *secundum se*, yet it does so in respect of its cause.

Excommunication is a punishment and a medicinal remedy; but punishments and medicinal remedies are administered as often as there is need, and so excommunications may be inflicted as often as there is due cause.

CCLXXXVIII. With persons excommunicated by the Lesser Excommunication, which separates only from participation of the Sacraments, and not from the fellowship of the faithful, it is lawful to communicate, although not to confer on such the Sacraments. But with persons excommunicated by the Greater Excommunication, which separates from the fellowship of the faithful as well as from Sacraments, it is not lawful to communicate.

Inasmuch, however, as the Church employs Excommunication to heal and not to slay, there are excepted from this general rule *certain matters* on which it is lawful to communicate—those, namely, which pertain to salvation. 2. *Certain persons* also are excepted, as the wife, the son (if not emancipated), the slave (if in bondage previous to the excommunication), and other dependants of the excommunicated person. 3. *Certain cases* also are excepted, as ignorance of the excommunication, the case of foreigners and travellers in the land of the excommunicated, who may lawfully buy from them, or even receive an alms. 4. Lastly, if any one see the excommunicated person in necessity, he is bound, by the precept of charity, to provide for him. These exceptions are contained in the verse:

Utile, lex, humile, res ignorata, necesse.

Utile refers to the words of salvation; *lex* to matrimony; *humile* to subjection or bondage; and the rest are obvious.

CCLXXXIX. If one is excommunicated, with all belonging to him, then there is no doubt that whosoever has fellowship with him is excommunicated by the Greater Excommunication. But one may be excommunicated *simpliciter*. In this case, if one have fellowship with him in his crime, by affording him counsel, aid, or favour, he is also excommunicated with the Greater Excommunication. If he have fellowship with him only in word, or by kiss, or at board, he is excommunicated with the Lesser Excommunication.

The Church does not intend to correct *unbelievers* in like manner as she does the faithful, the cure of whom is incumbent upon her; and so she does not debar her members from their society, as she does from the society of those of the faithful whom she has excommunicated.

CCXC. He only sins *mortally* by having fellowship with an excommunicated person who partakes with him in his crime, or *in divinis*, or in contempt of the Church.

CCXCI. From the Lesser Excommunication any one can absolve, who can absolve from the sin of participation? But if it be the Greater Excommunication, it has either been imposed by a judge, and then only he who imposed it, or his superior, can take it off: or it has been imposed by the law, and, if so, a bishop or even a priest can loose it, with the exception of six cases, which the Lawgiver, to wit, the Pope, has reserved to himself—1. When any one lays hands on a clerk or a religious. 2. When one breaks into a Church, and has been denounced. 3. When one burns a Church, and has been denounced. 4. When one knowingly communicates *in divinis* with another who has been excommunicated *nominaliter* by the Pope. 5. When one falsifies Letters of the Apostolic See. 6. When one communicates in his crime with an excommunicated person.

To the first case there are eight exceptions—1. If he be *in articulo mortis*, in which case any person soever may be loosed from any excommunication whatsoever, by any priest whomsoever. 2. If he be the door-keeper of any person in power, and have struck, not from hatred, or malicious purpose. 3. If the striker be a woman. 4. If the striker be a slave whose lord is not to blame, and would suffer loss by his absence. 5. If a regular strike a regular, unless the excess be enormous. 6. If the striker be a pauper. 7. If he be beneath the age of puberty, or an old man, or a valetudinarian. 8. If he have deadly enmities.

There are also seven other cases in which one who strikes a clerk does not incur excommunication therefor—1. If he strike for the purpose of discipline, as a master or prelate. 2. If in jocose levity. 3. If he find him working wickedness with his wife, or mother, or sister, or daughter. 4. If he immediately repel force by force. 5. If the one be ignorant that the other is a clerk. 6. If he find him in apostasy after the third admonition. 7. If the clerk have taken to a course of action wholly contrary to his profession, as, if he has become a soldier or a bigamist.

CCXCII. The evil of guilt differs from the evil of pain in this, that the very principle of guilt is the voluntariness of the sin, while, on the other hand, the very principle of punishment is its involuntary nature. It follows that, as sins cannot be committed against the will, so they cannot be remitted against the will; but as excommunication, which is a punishment, may be inflicted against the will, so even against the will may it be taken off.

CCXCIII. Excommunications have no necessary connection with each other; and so it is possible for a man to be absolved from one excommunication, and yet remain in another.

Sometimes a man has been excommunicated with divers excommunications by one judge; and then, if he be absolved from one, he is understood to be absolved from all, unless the contrary be expressed. But if the various excommunications have been inflicted by divers judges, the absolution of one judge does not affect the excommunications of the others, unless it be confirmed by them.

As one may be separated from the Church by many causes, so one cause of separation may be removed, the others remaining.

CCXCIV. It is granted on all hands that Indulgences are of some value, for it would be impious to say that the Church does aught in vain.

But some say that they do not avail to absolution from liability to that punishment which every one, according to the judgment of God, merits in purgatory, but avail only to absolution from the obligation whereby the priest bound the penitent to the performance of a certain penance, or to which he was bound under the provisions of the Canons. This opinion, however, does not appear to be a true one, in the first place, since it contradicts the privilege expressly given to Peter, that whatsoever he should loose on earth should be loosed in heaven—whence a remission made at the bar of the Church is valid also at the bar of God. Besides, did the Church grant indulgences of this sort, she would rather hurt than help, inasmuch as she would reserve to the more grievous pains of purgatory, by absolving from the penance enjoined to be done on earth. It is, therefore, to be taught and believed that Indulgences avail, both at the bar of the Church and at the bar of God, to the remission of the residue of punishment remaining due after contrition, confession, and absolution, whether enjoined or not.

CCXCV. The *rationale* of the value of indulgences is to be found in the unity of the Mystical Body of Christ. Many members of that Body have, in their works of penance, exceeded the due measure of their debts. Many have patiently endured unjust tribulations, whereby a multitude of penalties would have been expiated, had they been due by the sufferers. Of these merits contributed by the various members of the One Body, there is such an abundance, that they exceed every punishment due by all now living; and then, besides, and over and above them, there are the inexhaustible merits of the Head of the Body—even Christ.

This treasury of merits is the common property of all the members of the One Body—that is to say, of the Church at large: as the Apostle, writing to the Colossians, says, I rejoice in my sufferings for you, and fill up that which is behind of the afflictions of Christ, in my flesh, for His Body's sake, which is the Church.

CCXCVI. The common property of the multitude is distributed to the individuals who compose it, according to their various needs, and according to the judgment of him who presides over them. Hence, as any one may obtain remission of the punishment due by him, if another specially satisfy for him, so may he, in like manner, if the general satisfactions of another be allotted to him.

An indulgence then is not, strictly speaking, so much an absolution from punishment, as a *gift of wherewithal to pay the debt* of punishment.

CCXCVII. It might be urged that the granting of indulgences would have a tendency to make men relax in their works of penance. It might, were they inordinately bestowed. All those who obtain indulgences are to be counselled that they do not on that account abstain from the enjoined works of penance. These works they would find to be remedial, even were they free from debt of punishment. Again, they are sometimes debtors for more than they themselves believe and know. Still further, we must ever remember that God's grace is a more powerful remedy in order to the avoidance of sin than our works; and the affection which the receiver of an indulgence conceives in his mind towards the cause of that indulgence, disposes to grace.

CCXCVIII. In order to the validity of an indulgence there must be present on the part of the granter, *authority;* on the part of the receiver, *charity;* while the cause of the grant must be pious, and embrace the honour of God and the welfare of man. An inordinate indulgence is valid, although he who grants it sins.

CCXCIX. Although indulgences are of great value in order to the remission of temporal punishment, yet other satisfactory works are more meritorious in respect of essential reward, which is infinitely better, and so more to be sought after, than merely the remission of temporal pains.

CCC. Things temporal are ordained in order to things spiritual, for on account of things spiritual we ought to use things temporal. And so for things simply temporal indulgences may not be granted, but they may for temporals ordained in order to spirituals; as, for instance, the repression of the enemies of the Church who disturb her peace, the building of churches and bridges, the bestowal of alms and other works of mercy. This is not Simony, which is the giving of spiritual things for temporal.

Aid so given, however, must be in proportion to the giver's means. A poor man's penny may gain an indulgence which a rich man's pounds will not procure. Witness the case of the widow's farthing.

CCCI. Indulgences have effect according as the satisfactory works of one are reckoned to another, not only by the force of charity, but by the intention of the worker being in some way directed towards the recipient. Now, one's intention may be directed towards another in three ways—generally, specially, and individually. *Individually,* as when one satisfies for another determinately, and, in this way, any one may communicate to another his works. *Specially,* as when one prays for his congregation, his friends, or benefactors, and so this also ordains his satisfactory works. So, he who is set over a congregation may communicate his works by applying his intention to those of whom it is composed. *Generally*, as when one ordains his works to the good of the Church in general. And so he who is set over the Church in general may communicate these works by applying his intention to this or that individual in particular.

CCCII. As in the whole Church only, and not in any single congregation, or collection of congregations, there exists an indeficiency or unfailing store of merits, consisting of the merits of the saintly members, but chiefly of the merits of the Man Christ, the Adorable Head of the One Body, so He only can grant indulgences who is set over not a single congregation, or collection of congregations, but the whole Church.

CCCIII. Congregations of men are twofold—*œconomical*, as of those who are of one family; or *political*, as of those who are of one people. The Church is like a political congregation—the gathering of many parishes into one diocese being like a congregation of many families into one people. A Bishop only is therefore properly called a prelate of the Church, and so he alone, as Spouse of the Church, receives a ring. He alone has full power in the dispensation of the sacraments, and jurisdiction *in foro* of causes as a publick person; but others according as it is committed to them by him. The priests who are set over the people are not prelates *simpliciter*, but, as it were, co-adjutors. And hence in the Consecration of Priests the Bishop says—The more fragile we are, the more stand we in need of these helps.

Parish Priests, Abbots, and other like prelates cannot, therefore, as such, grant indulgences.

CCCIV. The power of granting indulgences is a consequent of the power of jurisdiction. But deacons and others, not priests, may have power of jurisdiction, either *committed* jurisdiction, as that of a legate; or *ordinary*, as that of a Bishop elect; and so they may grant indulgences, although they cannot absolve at the bar of penance—such absolution being a consequent of order.

CCCV. The Pope has the plenitude of pontifical power as a king in a kingdom, while the Bishops are assumed to a share of his solicitude, as judges are placed over separate communities, on which account the Pope styles them, and them alone, his brethren, calling all other men his sons. And so the power of granting indulgences resides primarily in the Pope, who for a legitimate cause can do what he wills. In bishops the power is limited according to the Pope's appointment.

CCCVI. Since by mortal sin a prelate does not lose his power of jurisdiction, he does not lose the power of granting indulgences.

An indulgence granted by a prelate in mortal sin is equally valid with an indulgence granted by the holiest of men; since the pain is remitted by virtue, not of the dispenser's merits, but of those laid up in the treasury of the Church.

CCCVII. A dead member cannot be influenced by the other living members. But a man in mortal sin is a dead member. And so he cannot by indulgence be influenced by the merits of other living members.

CCCVIII. To no one can the punishment of the sin be remitted to whom the guilt of the sin has not been remitted; and so indulgences are granted only in favour of those who, being truly contrite, have made confession of their sins.

CCCIX. The cause being removed, the effect is removed. If, therefore, one does not do that for which the indulgence is given, which is the cause of the indulgence, he does not acquire the indulgence. Again, the merits are applied or communicated by the intention of him who grants the indulgence; but the intention of him who grants is that the condition be performed.

CCCX. An indulgence ought to be granted for some cause whereby one may be provoked to an act tending to the glory of God, or the good of the Church; but a prelate, to whom the good of the Church and the furtherance of the Divine honour has been specially committed, has no cause to provoke himself thereto. Nevertheless, he may avail himself of indulgences instituted for others with these causes, as otherwise he would be in worse case than they.

CCCXI. Publick and solemn penance is sometimes enjoined for publick and very grievous crimes, and that for four reasons. 1. That a publick sin may have a publick remedy. 2. Because he deserves, even in this world, very grievous confusion who has committed a very grievous crime. 3. As a terror to others. 4. As an example of doing penance, that those who have fallen into grievous sins may not despair.

CCCXII. Public penitents may not receive Holy Orders. They are not even to receive minor orders, unless necessity or custom allow, and then by dispensation. In no case are they to be promoted to Sacred Orders. 1. By reason of the dignity of these orders. 2. From fear of relapse. 3. For avoidance of scandal to those in whose memories the publick penance yet remains. 4. Because they whose sin had been such would not have the face to rebuke others.

CCCXIII. Solemn Penance may not be iterated for three reasons—1, lest it thereby become common; 2, by reason of its signification of the expulsion of the first man from Paradise, which was done but once; 3, because the solemnity is, as it were, a profession of perpetual penance. With this idea iteration would interfere.

If the publick penitent sin again, a place of repentance is still open; only a solemn penance is not again enjoined.

CCCXIV. Every solemn penance is publick: but not conversely, is every publick penance solemn. A solemn penance is on this wise:—on the first day of Lent, *in capite Quadragesimae*, the penitents present themselves with their priests to the Bishop at the Church doors, clothed in sackcloth, their feet bare, their eyes cast on the ground, and, if men, with their hair cut off. Being led into the Church, the Bishop and all the clergy say the vii. penitential psalms. He then lays his hands on them, sprinkles them with holy water, puts ashes on their heads, covers their necks with haircloth, and with tears proclaims that, as Adam was driven from Paradise, so are they cast out of the Church. He then orders the ministers to drive them out of the Church, the clergy following them with this Responsory; In the sweat of thy face, &c. On Maundy Thursday in every year, they are brought back to the Church by their priests, and there remain till the Octave of Easter, but neither communicate nor receive the (blessed) bread. And so will they do every year as long as an entrance to the Church is forbidden them. The final reconciliation is reserved to the Bishop, to whom alone the imposition of solemn penance pertains.

Solemn Penance may be imposed both on men and women, but not on clerks, to avoid scandal. Such penance, moreover, ought not to be imposed, save for a sin which has made a commotion in the whole place.

A publick, but not solemn, Penance is one done in face of the Church, but not with the foresaid solemnities, as a pilgrimage through the world with an ellwand. Such a penance may be iterated, may be imposed by a simple priest, and may even be enjoined on a clerk.

6. The Sacrament of Extreme Unction.

CCCXV. OF the visible operations of the Church, some are sacraments, as Baptism; others, as Exorcism, are sacramentals. Between these two, a Sacrament and a Sacramental, there is this difference. That action of the Church is called a *Sacrament* which attains to the effect principally intended in the administration of the Sacraments; while that action is called a *Sacramental*, which, although it does not attain to that effect, is yet in a way ordained in order to that principal action. Now the effect intended in the administration of the Sacraments is the healing of the disease of sin. But Extreme Unction, as appears from the words of S. James, is ordained to produce this effect; and, moreover, is not ordained in order to, or annexed to any other Sacrament, and so is not merely a Sacramental, but itself a Sacrament.

CCCXVI. This Sacrament immediately disposes a man to glory, being given to those who are departing from the body. Now, under the old law the estate of glory had not yet arrived, for as S. Paul says, the law led to nothing perfect, and so this Sacrament was not therein prefigured by any figure of the same *genus* corresponding thereto, although it was, in a way, by certain *remote* figures, to wit, by the various healings read of in the Old Testament.

CCCXVII. Extreme Unction, although it be effected by many actions, is nevertheless *one* Sacrament, since these actions are all ordained to signify and effect one reality (res). The healing of the many and diverse spiritual wounds cannot be perfectly signified save by application of the medicine to the various roots of these wounds.

CCCXVIII. As to the institution of Extreme Unction by Christ or otherwise, opinions are twofold. Some say, that this Sacrament and that of Confirmation, Christ did not institute by Himself, but gave to be instituted by His Apostles, inasmuch as these two, by reason of the plenitude of grace which is conferred in them, could not be instituted before the plenary mission of the Holy Ghost. But this reasoning has but little cogency; for as Christ, before His Passion, promised the plenary mission of the Holy Ghost, so could He also have instituted these two Sacraments. Others say that Christ Himself instituted all the Sacraments, but that some, and those most difficult of belief, He promulgated by Himself, and others, as Confirmation and Extreme Unction, He reserved to be promulgated by His Apostles. And this seems to be the more probable opinion, because the Sacraments pertain to the foundation of the law, and so their institution pertains to the Lawgiver. And again, because the Sacraments have their efficacy of their institution, and this they would not have, were it not divine.

CCCXIX. The Lord said and did many things which are not contained in the Gospels. The Evangelists were chiefly careful to hand down a tradition of those things which belong to the necessity of salvation, or the due disposing of the Church; and so they have narrated the institution by Christ of Baptism, Penance, the Eucharist, and Order, rather than of Confirmation and Extreme Unction, both of which are neither of necessity to salvation, nor belong to the due ordering, distinguishing, and disposing of the Church.

There is, however, mention made in the Gospel of anointing with oil, for S. Mark relates, That the Twelve, when sent forth by Jesus, went out and preached that men should repent, and cast out many devils, and *anointed with oil many that were sick*, and healed them.

CCCXX. True, the Master of the Sentences says that Extreme Unction was instituted *ab Apostolis;* but the Angelical Doctor holds that he so said because by the teaching of the Apostles its institution has been promulgated to us.

CCCXXI. The Sacraments of the New Law are of greater dignity than were the Sacraments of the Old. But all the Sacraments of the Old Law were divinely instituted. Therefore and à *fortiori* all the Sacraments of the New.

CCCXXII. That spiritual healing which is exhibited for the last time ought to be *perfect*, since after it there remains no other; and also *gentle*, in order that the hope which is most necessary for the departing be not shattered but fostered. Now, oil is lenitive, and penetrating, even to the inwards, and also diffusive; and so, for both of the reasons foresaid, is the fit matter of this sacrament.

When Oil is spoken of, Oil of Olives is meant, other liquors being called oil simply from their resemblance to it.

Although Oil of Olives does not grow everywhere, yet it may be easily transported to any place; and besides, this sacrament is not like Baptism, of so great necessity that those going hence without it, could not attain salvation.

CCCXXIII. This sacrament consists in the anointing, as Baptism does in the washing: and the matter of this sacrament is sanctified oil. A threefold reason may be assigned why there is required in this and in certain other sacraments, sanctification of the matter. 1. All the efficacy of the sacraments descends from Christ. Those sacraments which He Himself used have efficacy from that use; as by the touch of His adorable Flesh, He conferred on water its generative power. But He did not use either this sacrament, or any other corporal anointing; and so in this as in all anointings there is required previous sanctification of the matter. 2. By reason of the plenitude of grace, which is bestowed to take away not only guilt, but also the relicks of sin, and bodily infirmity. 3. Its corporal effect, namely, bodily healing is not caused by the natural properties of the matter; and so this efficacy must be given to it by its sanctification.

CCCXXIV. As in other anointings the matter is consecrated by a Bishop, so ought it to be also in this: in this as in them to make manifest that the sacerdotal power is derived from the Episcopal.

The efficacy of the Sacraments descends from Christ, in Whom it primarily resides as has been shewn, to His people in due order. It descends to them by means, that is, through the mediation of His ministers who dispense His sacraments, and to His inferior ministers through the mediation of their rulers whom He has set over them, and who sanctify the matter. In all sacraments, therefore, which require sanctified matter, its first sanctification is effected by the Bishop, although its use be in some of them committed to the priest, and this to show that the sacerdotal power is derived from the episcopal, according to the Psalm: It is like the precious ointment upon the Head, that is, Christ, that (first) ran down unto the beard, even unto Aaron's beard, that is, the Episcopate, and went down to the skirts of His clothing, that is, the Priesthood.

The Sacrament of the Eucharist consists in the sanctification, not in the use of the matter. Properly speaking, therefore, that which is the matter of that Sacrament is not anything consecrated, and so there is not required any previous sanctification of its matter by a Bishop. There is, however, a sanctification of the altar and its belongings, and also of the priest himself. This cannot be effected save by a Bishop; and so it is again made manifest that the sacerdotal power is derived from the episcopal.

As regards the Very (Verum) Body of Christ, there is no order above the priesthood; but as regards the Mystical Body of Christ, the episcopal order is above the sacerdotal.

CCCXXV. Every sacrament effects by signifying; but the signification of the matter is not determined in order to its effect (for it might have relation to many things), save by a determinate form of words; and so in all the Sacraments of the New Law, which effect what they figure, there must be both realities and words (res et verba). Besides, S. James seems to place the whole force of this Sacrament in prayer, which is its form.

Holy Scripture is proposed to all men *communiter;* and so the form of Baptism which may be given by all is therein set forth, and so in like manner is the form of the Eucharist, which expresses the faith concerning that Sacrament which is of necessity to salvation. But the forms of the other sacraments are not found delivered in the Sacred Scriptures; the Church has them from the tradition of the Apostles, who received them from the Lord; as the Apostle said to the Corinthians: I have received of the Lord that which also I delivered unto you.

CCCXXVI. The form of this Sacrament is *deprecative prayer*, as appears from the words of S. James, and from the use of the Roman Church, which uses only deprecative words in conferring this Sacrament. For this manifold reasons are assigned. 1. The receiver of this Sacrament is destitute of his own proper powers, and so needs to be supported by prayers. 2. It is administered to the departing, as they are on the point of leaving the bar of the Church to rest in the hand of God alone. To Him they are committed by prayer. 3.

This Sacrament has not any effect, such as invariably follows *ex operatione* of the minister in other sacraments, their essentials having been duly attended to, as *character* in baptism and confirmation, the transubstantiation in the Eucharist, and remission of sin in Penance, consequent on the existence of contrition, contrition being of the essence of penance. It is not of the essence of this sacrament, and so the form of this sacrament cannot, as in the case of the foresaid sacraments, be in the indicative mood.

In some churches indicative words are said as, I anoint these eyes with holy oil, in the name of the Father, &c., but these are not formal words. They are only dispositive to the form, which consists in the deprecative words, By this holy anointing, and by His most piteous mercy the Lord pardon thee, whereinsoever thou hast done amiss by seeing, &c. This form is used as comprehending: 1. The Sacrament—by this holy anointing; 2. What operates in the Sacrament—the Divine Mercy; 3. And its effect—the remission of sins.

CCCXXVII. Every sacrament has been instituted principally to produce one special effect, although it may produce, as consequences, other effects besides. But the sacraments effect what they figure. And so from their signification is to be ascertained their principal effect. This Sacrament is administered by way of medicine, as baptism is by way of washing. But medicine is intended for the removal of infirmity. And so this sacrament has been instituted *principally* in order to heal the infirmity of sin. Hence, as Baptism is a spiritual regeneration, and Penance a spiritual resuscitation, so is Extreme Unction a spiritual curing or healing. Now, as corporal healing presupposes corporal life, so does spiritual healing presuppose spiritual life; and so this Sacrament is not ordained to remedy those defects whereby spiritual life is taken away—that is to say, is not ordained against original sin, or mortal sin—but to remedy those defects whereby a man is made spiritually infirm, and deprived of perfect vigour to perform the acts of the life, whether of grace or of glory. This defect is neither more nor less than a debility and inaptitude, which is left in man by sin, whether original or actual. Against this debility a man is strengthened by this Sacrament. Grace, however, cannot suffer the coexistence of sin, and so, if it find any sin, whether mortal or venial, it takes it away *quoad culpam*, if so be that no obstacle is interposed on the part of the recipient. This has been already shown with regard to Confirmation and the Eucharist.

The *principal* effect, therefore, of Extreme Unction, is the removal of the relicks of sin, which constitute the aforesaid debility; its *consequential* effect is the remission *quoad culpam*, of any sin it may find in the soul.

CCCXXVIII. This may seem, at first sight, to preclude the necessity of Penance, but it is not so. Although the principal effect of a sacrament may be had without actual reception of that sacrament, or without a sacrament, or by means of the consequential effects of another sacrament—yet it is never had without a purpose of receiving the sacrament, whose principal effect it is. And so, as Penance has been instituted principally against actual guilt, any other sacrament destroys actual guilt only consequentially, and does not thereby exclude the necessity of Penance.

CCCXXIX. Extreme Unction remits sin, as to its stain, as to its *reatus* of punishment, and as to its relicks. 1. Guilt, as to its stain, is not remitted without contrition, but this sacrament, by the grace which it infuses, causes the motion of the free will towards sin to be contrition: as may occur also in Confirmation and the Eucharist. 2. Similarly also it diminishes the *reatus* of temporal punishment, but *ex consequenti*, inasmuch as it removes the debility, for to a strong man the pain is less grievous than to a weak man. And so the measure of satisfaction is not diminished; on the contrary, the sick man is bound, on his convalescence to perform the satisfaction enjoined. 3. There remain in the soul of the sick man certain dispositions, the relicks of previous acts of sin, as is plain on his convalescence, but these are certain inchoate habits, and not what are commonly called the relicks of sin, which consist in a spiritual debility existing in the mind itself. It being taken away, even although these same habits or dispositions remain, the mind cannot be so easily inclined to sin.

CCCXXX. As Baptism, by a bodily washing, effects a spiritual cleansing from spiritual stains, so this sacrament, by an external sacramental medication effects a spiritual healing of spiritual wounds. As the washing of baptism has the effect also of bodily washing in that it effects also bodily cleansing; so Extreme Unction has in like manner the effect of bodily remedies, to wit, bodily healing. But there is this difference. Bodily washing effects bodily cleansing from the natural properties of the element of water, and so always effects it; but Extreme Unction does not effect bodily healing from the natural properties of its matter, but from the Divine virtue, which operates according to reasonable causes. Since the reason operating never induces a *secondary* effect, unless it be expedient for the furtherance of the *principal* effect, so there does not always follow from this sacrament bodily healing, its secondary effect, but only when it is expedient for the furtherance of its principal effect— spiritual healing. In that case it always follows, if so be that no impediment be interposed on the part of the recipient.

CCCXXXI. *Character* is not imprinted save in those sacraments whereby a man is destined to the performance or to the reception of somewhat sacred. But this sacrament is solely for a remedy; and so does not confer *character*. No sacrament imprinting *character* is iterated; but Extreme Unction may be iterated: and so does not confer *character*.

The distinction of sacramental *character* is a distinction effected among those who are in the Church of the present; but Extreme Unction is conferred on those only who are departing from the Church of the present. It does not therefore imprint *character*.

The sacramental *character* conferred in Baptism, Confirmation, and Order marks the recipients of these Sacraments according to the states of life on which they, by their reception of them, severally enter, as the children, the soldiers, and the ministers of Christ. But there is no distinction, in estate of life, between the anointed and the unanointed.

In every sacrament, as has been said, there is somewhat which is *res* only, somewhat which is *sacramentum* only, and somewhat also which is both *res* and *sacramentum*. That which, in this Sacrament is both *res and sacramentum* is, not *character*, but a certain inward devotion, which is spiritual unction.

CCCXXXII. Although a laic may administer Baptism, the sacrament of necessity, *in articulo mortis*, that the way of life be barred to no man, yet he cannot administer Extreme Unction, which is not a sacrament of so great necessity as to require such a dispensation.

A laic is but a private person, and so, if unworthy, his prayer would not be heard; but the prayers in this Sacrament are made by the priest as a publick person, that is to say, they are offered by him in the person of the whole Church, and not in his own.

Moreover, in this Sacrament there is made a remission of sin; and laics have no power of remitting sins.

CCCXXXIII. Deacons have purgative power only and not illuminative. Those sacraments are illuminative in which grace is conferred. And so no sacrament which confers grace can a Deacon *ex officio* minister. He ministers baptism not *ex officio*, but *ex necessitate*.

S. James says: Is any sick among you? Let him call for the elders (presbyteros) that is, *the priests* of the Church, and let them pray over him, anointing him with oil, in the name of the Lord. And the prayer of faith shall save the sick, and the Lord shall raise him up; and, if he have committed sins, they shall be forgiven him.

CCCXXXIV. According to Dionysius, the office proper and peculiar to a Bishop is to perfect, as that of a Priest is to illuminate. And so there is reserved to Bishops only the dispensation of those sacraments which place the receiver in an estate of perfection above his fellows. But this sacrament is given to all, and so may be ministered by simple priests.

The sick man, according to the Apostolic injunction, is to call for the ministers of this Sacrament. But a Bishop could not possibly come to all the sick of his diocese; he therefore is evidently not, or *quâ* Bishop, the sole minister of this sacrament.

CCCXXXV. This Sacrament being a spiritual healing, signified and effected by means of bodily healing, may be conferred on those only to whom bodily healing is competent, that is, on the sick only, and not on the whole. This is analogous to the case of Baptism, which, as a spiritual washing, signified and effected by means of bodily washing, may be conferred on those only to whom bodily washing is competent, as, for instance, not on a child within its mother's womb.

Baptism pertains to those who are entering on this world, Extreme Unction to those who are departing from it: but to those only who are departing from it by natural death, and whose departure might be stayed by bodily healing. For instance, Extreme Unction is not to be administered to one about to leave this world by being beheaded.

CCCXXXVI. This Sacrament, as its name imports—Extreme Unction, or the Last Anointing—is the last remedy which the Church can confer, as immediately disposing the soul to glory: and so is not to be administered to every sick person, but to those only who are in peril of death, their sickness being sufficiently grievous to cause death, and so to be their last.

CCCXXXVII. This Sacrament is not to be administered to furious persons or idiots.—1. To avoid irreverence; 2. because the receivers' faith and devotion chiefly avail in order to their reception of its effect. These are lacking on the part of such persons, save during lucid intervals, when it may be administered to them.

CCCXXXVIII. This Sacrament requires actual devotion on the part of its receivers as does the Eucharist; and as on this account the Eucharist is not given to children, so neither on the same account is there administered to them Extreme Unction.

Again, this Sacrament is to be administered to no one to whom its formal words do not apply. They do not apply to children who have not sinned, for instance, by seeing or hearing as the form implies. Further, Extreme Unction is a remedy directed principally against actual sin and its relicks, not against original sin and the *fomes* remaining after its remission.

CCCXXXIX. As in bodily healing so in spiritual, there is anointed not the whole body, but those parts only which contain the roots of the spiritual malady.

Although, as S. Augustine teaches, the soul be *tota in toto corpore, tota quoque in ejus quâlibet parte*, as to its essence, it is not so present as to its powers, which are the roots of the acts of sin. And so the remedy is applied to the determinate parts in which these powers of the soul have their being and residence.

CCCXL. The principles of sinning are the same in us as the principles of acting, because sin consists in action. Now, the principles of acting in us are three in number. 1. That which directs—the *cognoscitive* power. 2. That which governs—the *appetitive* power. 3. That which executes—the *motive* power. All our cognitions have their rise from our senses, and because where there is in us the first origin of sin, there ought the medicine to be applied, so there are anointed the local residences of the five senses—to wit, the eyes for seeing; the ears for hearing; the nostrils for smelling; the mouth for taste; the hands for touch—which chiefly resides in the fleshy portions of the fingers. For the *appetitive* the reins are by some anointed. The feet are anointed for the *motive*, as being its principal instruments. Because the first principle of human operation is the *cognoscitive*, that unction is observed by all as of sacramental necessity, which has reference to the five senses. But some do not observe the others; and of these some anoint the feet and not the reins; and this because the *appetitive* and the *motive* are but *secondary* principles.

Membra genitalia propter immunditiam illarum partium, et honestatem sacramenti non debent inungi.

Mutilated persons are to be anointed as near as possible to those parts which ought to have been anointed, because, although those members are awanting, there are not awanting those powers of the soul which have their usual residence therein; and by means of them the mutilated person may sin inwardly, albeit not outwardly.

CCCXLI. As bodily healing may be iterated, so also may spiritual. Extreme Unction then, as not producing a perpetual effect, may be iterated, but not during the progress of the same disease.

7. THE SACRAMENT OF ORDER.

CCCXLII. THE estate of the Church stands midway between the estate of nature and the estate of glory. In nature is found an order whereby some are superior to others; so also in grace, as appears by the hierarchy of the angels; and therefore it is meet that in the Church there should be a sacred order whereby some should be set over others for the benefit of others, and not for their own.

CCCXLIII. Order is an outward sign whereby spiritual power is delivered to the ordained. It is therefore a sacrament.

CCCXLIV. Since the perfection of the Divine works requires that to whomsoever there is divinely given any power, there should be given also those things which are necessary in order to its due execution; there is given in the Sacrament of Order grace *gratum faciens*, in order that the ordained may worthily dispense the sacraments.

The Sacraments of the New Law effect what they signify. The septenary number of Orders signifies the seven gifts of the Holy Ghost which the Orders also convey.

CCCXLV. Since by every order, minor as well as sacred, a man is constituted above the people in a degree of power ordained in order to the dispensation of the Sacraments, *character*, a distinctive sign marking him off from all others, is imprinted by every order.

As in Baptism and Confirmation, so also in Order character is indelible, and therefore the Sacrament which confers it cannot be iterated. Even if a man be deprived of, or abandon his office, his *character* still remains; as is apparent by this that when he is restored or returns to his office he is not re-ordained.

CCCXLVI. No man can receive aught who has not in him receptive power, and so the character of Order presupposes the *character* of Baptism, which is the gate of the sacraments and gives man power to receive them. If an unbaptised person be promoted to the priesthood he is not a priest; he can neither consecrate the Body and Blood of Christ, nor can he absolve in the tribunal of penance. He is, according to the Canons, to be baptised and re-ordained. If he have been promoted to the Episcopate, those whom he ordains have no orders. Yet it may be piously believed, that, as to the ultimate effects of the Sacraments, the Great High Priest would supply the defect, and not suffer His Church to sustain so great a loss; nay, further, that He would not suffer the matter to lie hid, so that she should be deceived, and incur so great peril.

CCCXLVII. Of congruity, but not of necessity, as with baptism, the character of order presupposes the character of confirmation.

The Apostles received power of order before the Ascension, when Jesus said to them, Receive ye the Holy Ghost; but they were confirmed after the Ascension by the coming of the Holy Ghost.

CCCXLVIII. It is not of necessity to the reception of the higher orders that one have first received the lower, their powers being distinct. In the primitive church some were ordained priests who had not received the inferior orders. They could nevertheless do all that the inferior orders could, the inferior order being comprehended in the superior, as are the senses in the intellect, and as is dukedom in kingdom. The Church however afterwards prescribed that men should not thereafter enter the higher orders who had not previously humbled themselves in the lower. A person ordained *per saltum* is not to be re-ordained: but those orders which have been omitted are to be supplied.

CCCXLIX. Holiness of life is necessary, in order to fulfilment of the Divine precept, but not in order to the validity of the Sacrament. One who approached in mortal sin to receive orders, would indeed receive them, although he would incur the crime of presumption.

No man of the seed of Aaron that had any blemish was to approach to offer the bread of his God, or to offer the offerings of the Lord made by fire : he was not to go in within the veil, nor come nigh unto the altar lest he should profane the sanctuary which the Lord had sanctified.

S. Jerome says, it would be for the destruction of the Church were laymen to be better than clerks. Let these then excel in word and deed those over whom they preside.

Those who in holy order are made *medii* between God and the people, ought to have a good conscience toward God and a good report among men.

CCCL. That knowledge only is required in order to the reception of any order, which is necessary in order to the due performance of the functions attached thereto. For instance, a reader must be able to read but not necessarily to understand, because it does not belong to him to explain the meaning of what he reads. A priest has two acts to perform; one, and that the principal, with regard to the Very Body of Christ: another, and that secondary, with regard to the Mystical Body of Christ. Some men are promoted to the priesthood however to whom is committed the first only, as religious to whom is not committed the cure of souls, and from the mouth of such priests the law is not sought. It is sufficient that they have such knowledge as is requisite for the due observance of those things which are necessary in order to the right celebration of the sacraments. But others, as Parish priests, are promoted to the other act also; and the lips of such priests should keep knowledge, seeing the people will seek the law at their mouth, for they are the messengers of the Lord of Hosts. They are not indeed required to have knowledge of the whole Scriptures, or to be versed in all difficult questions, but they ought to be instructed in those matters of faith and morals which the people must believe, observe and do. To the Bishops and superior clergy belong the solution of intricate and difficult questions. S. Peter says, Be ready always to give an answer to every man that asketh you a reason of the hope that is in you, that is to say, such a ground of probability as properly belongs to the subject matter of faith which concerns the invisible, with regard to which real proof is impossible.

CCCLI. Although the ornament of holiness exceedingly becomes those who are to be or have been ordained, yet it does not *per se* advance any one to orders.

It belongs to Christ to give grace, in Whom is the fulness of grace, and from Whom it descends upon all men: it belongs to His ministers to give, not grace, but the sacraments of grace. And so orders are conferred, not by the possession of grace *per se*, but by reception of a *sacrament* of grace. Not every priest is holy, but every holy man is a priest, says Chrysostom, in that sense in which all just persons are kings and priests unto God. Holiness once had may be lost, but orders once had can never be lost.

CCCLII. The Lord said, Who is that faithful and wise steward whom his Lord shall make ruler over His Household, to give them their portion of meat in due season? He is guilty of unfaithfulness who gives to any one divine things above his measure, and this he does who promotes to orders an unworthy person, as that steward would be reckoned unfaithful to an earthly lord who promoted to office an unworthy servant. By good ministers God's honour and the Church's well-being are increased; by evil ministers both suffer loss.

God never so deserts His Church, but that there will will be found fit ministers in numbers sufficient for the necessities of the people: and if there were not so many found as there are now, it would be better, as S. Clement says, to have a few good ministers than many bad ones.

Bishops, to avoid all peril of unfaithfulness, ought to make diligent inquisition as to the knowledge and morals of those who approach them for orders. S. Paul counselled Timothy, Lay hands suddenly on no man.

CCCLIII. Since it is of the Natural Law, which cannot be dispensed, that holy things be holily handled, whosoever existing in mortal sin, does, except in extreme necessity, use the order he has received, sins mortally.

CCCLIV. The Church, the Mystical Body of Christ, consists, like the natural body, of many members, and these members have diverse offices. For the due performance of these there are ordained in the Church diverse orders.

The Mystery of the New Testament is more noble than was that of the Old. But in the Old Testament there were consecrated not only the priests, but also their ministers the Levites. And so *a fortiori* in the New Testament there ought to be, as there are, consecrated by the Sacrament of Order, not only priests, but also their various ministers.

A multiplicity of orders has been instituted in the Church for three reasons. 1. To commend the Wisdom of God, which most shiningly manifests itself in the distinctions of things, both natural and spiritual, which He has ordained. This is signified in what is recorded of the Queen of Sheba, that when she saw the order of the ministers of Solomon, there was no more spirit in her, being lost in admiration of the greatness of his wisdom. 2. For the relief and support of man's infirmity, for all the things which pertain to the divine mysteries, could not without great inconvenience be fulfilled by one. And so to perform diverse offices are ordained diverse orders. This was foreshadowed in the Old Law, when God gave to Moses seventy men of the elders of Israel, and put His Spirit upon them, that they might bear the burden of the people with him, that he should not bear it himself alone. 3. In order to give opportunity to a greater number to become fellow-workers with God, than which, as Dionysius says, there is nothing more divine.

CCCLV. The Sacrament of Order is ordained in order to the Sacrament of the Eucharist, which is the Sacrament of Sacraments. For as the temple and altar, and vessels and vestments, so also do the ministers who assist at the Eucharist need consecration; and the consecration of them is the Sacrament of Order. The distinction of the orders is to be viewed with regard to their several relations to the Eucharist, because the power of order is—1, either in order to the consecration of the Eucharist itself; or, 2, to some ministry connected therewith. i. If in order to the Consecration of the Eucharist, the Order is that of the Priesthood; and so when priests are ordained, and receive power to consecrate the Body and Blood of Christ, they have delivered to them a chalice with wine, and a paten with bread. ii. The co-operation of ministers has regard either, 1, to the Sacrament itself, or, 2, to its receivers. If it has regard to the Sacrament itself, it is threefold. 1. There is the ministry of dispensation. It pertains to the Deacon to dispense, although not to consecrate, the Precious Blood. 2. There is the ministry of ordering the matter of the Sacrament in the Holy Vessels. This belongs to the Sub-deacon, who carries the Holy Vessels, and places the Oblations on the Altar: in token whereof he receives from the hands of the Bishop, when he is ordained, a chalice, but empty. 3. There is the ministry of presenting the matter of the Sacrament. This belongs to the Acolyte, who prepares the cruetts with wine and water. He receives at Ordination a cruett, empty. iii. The ministries which relate to the receivers of the Sacrament, are also three in number, corresponding to the condition of unfit receivers, which is threefold. 1. Some are altogether unbelieving, and unwilling to believe. Such are to be wholly excluded from the vision of divine mysteries, and from the company of the faithful. The ministry of exclusion belongs to the Porters or Doorkeepers, *ostiarii*. 2. Some again are not unwilling to believe, but are not yet instructed. These are the Catechumens. For their instruction is ordained the order of Readers, to whom is committed the reading of the Old Testament, the first rudiments of the doctrine of the faith. 3. Others are faithful both as believers and as instructed, but are still under the power of demons. These are the Energumens, to minister to whom is appointed the order of Exorcists.

In accordance, therefore, with the number of ministries required for the due consecration and reverent handling of the Eucharist, seven orders have been instituted—to wit, 1. Priests; 2. Deacons; 3. Subdeacons; 4. Acolytes; 5. Readers; 6. Exorcists; 7. Doorkeepers.

CCCLVI. Some have seen in this distinction of orders an adaptation to those graces *gratis datae*, whereof S. Paul writes to the Corinthians. 1. The word of wisdom as belonging to the Bishop, as the ordainer of others, a function which pertains to wisdom. 2. The word of knowledge to the Priest, who ought to have the key of knowledge. 3. Faith to the Deacon, who proclaims the Gospel. 4. Working of miracles to the Subdeacon, who begins to aspire to works of perfection, by his vow of continence. 5. Interpretation of tongues to the Acolyte, which is signified by the light which he carries. 6. The grace of healing to the Exorcist. 7. Divers kinds of tongues to the Psalmist. 8. Prophecy to the Reader. 9. Discerning of spirits to the Doorkeepers, who exclude some and admit others. But two of these, Bishops and Psalmists, are not special orders, for, 1. Neither have any special relation to the sacrament of the Eucharist, as above shewn, and, 2. Psalmist or Chanter is a name common to every member of the choir, to every individual member of which it belongs to chant the psalms.

CCCLVII. Others have seen in the ordination of the Ecclesiastical hierarchy as of the celestial hierarchy, an adaptation to the three hierarchical acts. 1. Purging. 2. Illuminating. 3. Perfecting: and have said that 1. The doorkeeper purges exteriorly, by segregating the good from the evil. 2. That the acolyte purges interiorly, in that by the light which he bears he signifies the dispelling of interior darkness. 3. That the exorcist purges both exteriorly and interiorly, in that he expels the devil who disturbs in both ways.

ii. As to the illumination of doctrine, that it is attained. 1. As to prophetical doctrine, by the Readers. 2. As to apostolical doctrine by the Subdeacons, and, 3. As to evangelical doctrine by the Deacons. iii. As to perfecting, that it belongs to priests. But this will not hold good, for, 1. To Bishops belongs perfecting. 2. To priests illuminating — but, 3. Purging to all ministers. The Bishop possesses the whole three powers; the Priest, two: the Deacon or Minister, and under this name are comprehended all the inferior ministers, one.

CCCLVIII. In the Primitive Church, by reason of the paucity of ministers, all the inferior ministries were committed to Deacons, in whose power all the foresaid powers were *implicitly* contained. When afterwards the Divine worship was developed„ they were *explicitly* committed to diverse and several officers.

CCCLIX. All the orders are *secundum se*, sacred, but by reason of the matter, which in the Priesthood, the Diaconate and the Subdiaconate is consecrated, and not in the others, they are rightly divided into sacred and nonsacred.

The Priesthood and the Diaconate immediately concern the Body and Blood of Christ; the Subdiaconate the Holy Vessels which contain them. They who handle holy things should themselves be holy and clean; and so the reception of these three orders not only impedes the contracting of matrimony, but destroys the contract. Reception of the four minor orders does neither.

CCCLX. The several orders are superior in dignity in order as they approach the nearer to the Sacrament of the Eucharist, for the due celebration, right reception, and reverent handling of which they are all and severally ordained.

CCCLXI. Since the principal act of a priest is to consecrate the Body and Blood of Christ, the sacerdotal character is rightly imprinted by the giving of the chalice, delivered with a certain determinate form of words.

The Bishop, in conferring orders, does two things :—1, he prepares the receivers for the reception of order, and 2, he delivers to them the power of order. He prepares them by—1, instruction in their duty, and 2, by certain acts which are three in number: 1, benediction; 2, laying on of hands; 3, unction. By benediction they are separated, made over and taken possession of for the Divine service, and so to all is given benediction. By laying on of hands is given the fullness of grace, whereby men are fitted for the greater functions. And so only on Priests and Deacons, to whom belongs, to the one as principal, to the other as minister, the dispensation of the Sacraments, are hands laid. Priests alone are anointed, who touch with their hands the Body of Christ, along with the Paten which contains It, and the Chalice which contains His Blood. Sacerdotal power is conferred, and sacerdotal character is impressed by the delivery of that which pertains to the principal and peculiar sacerdotal act.

CCCLXII. The Lord gave His disciples the sacerdotal powers as to the principal act, before the Passion in the Supper, when He said, Take, eat, adding, Do this in remembrance of me. But after His Resurrection He gave them the sacerdotal power as to its secondary act, which is to bind and loose, when He said, Receive ye the Holy Ghost; whosesoever sins ye remit, they are remitted unto them, and whosesoever sins ye retain they are retained.

CCCLXIII. As the Bishop, by reason of the more excellent power which he has, alone confirms, consecrates virgins, and stations others in the various offices of the Divine Ministry, so to him alone also it belongs to confer Holy Orders.

CCCLXIV. The sacerdotal *character* is not given by the laying on of hands, as above set forth, but grace is given in order to the execution of the functions of the order, and because men therefore need the most ample graces, the assisting priests, along with the Bishop, lay their hands on those who are to be promoted to the priesthood. On deacons the Bishop alone lays his hands.

CCCLXV. The Pope, who possesses the plenitude of Pontifical power, can commit to one who is not a Bishop such things pertaining to the Episcopal dignity as have no immediate relation to the Very Body of Christ. And so, by commission from him, any simple priest can confer the minor orders and confirm, but not a person who is not a priest. But a priest cannot confer the greater orders, which have immediate relation to the Body of Christ, over the consecrating of Which the Pope has no greater power than a simple priest.

CCCLXVI. Heretical Bishops, and Bishops cut off from the communion of the Church, since they can never lose the power once given them with their consecration, can confer holy orders as they can celebrate other sacraments; but those ordained by them have no power to execute their offices, nor do they receive grace—not by reason of the inefficiency of the sacraments, but by reason of their own sin, who receive them contrary to the prohibition of the Church.

Those cut off from the Church have no power of jurisdiction, and so cannot absolve, absolution depending on such power.

The power given to a Bishop in his promotion perpetually remains in him, although it cannot be called *character*, because a man is not thereby ordained directly to God, but to the Mystical Body of Christ, and yet it remains indelibly as does *character*, because it is given by consecration, which belongs to a thing, as even to an altar or vessel, as long as the thing itself exists.

CCCLXVII. There are certain things required in the receiver of a sacrament as *of necessity to the sacrament*; and if they be wanting, the receiver can receive neither the Sacrament nor its reality—neither the *Sacramentum*, nor the *Res Sacramenti*. But there are certain other things required, not as of necessity to the sacrament, but of necessity *by reason of precept*, on account of their congruity to the sacrament. Without these one does indeed receive the *Sacramentum*, but not the *Res Sacramenti*. Now, in order to the reception of orders, there is required the masculine sex, by reason not only of the second necessity, but of the first also. And so, if to a woman there be done all those things which are done in orders, she yet does not receive orders. A sacrament is a sign, and must contain not only a reality (*res*), but must signify the same. Now, in the feminine sex, there cannot be signified any eminency of degree, because the estate of a woman is to be in subjection, and so she is not susceptive of order, which implies such eminency.

S. Paul writes to Timothy, Let the woman learn in silence with all subjection. I suffer not a woman to teach, nor to usurp authority over the man, but to be in silence. For Adam was first formed, then Eve.

The *corona*, or tonsure, precedes ordination, although it is not of necessity to the Sacrament; but this is not competent to a woman, for it is a shame for a woman to be shorn or shaven.

CCCLXVIII. Childhood, which does not possess, and other defects which take away the use of reason, are impediments in the way of *action*. Persons, therefore, thus situated or so afflicted, cannot receive sacraments which require *action* on the part of their receivers, as Penance, Matrimony, or the like. But *infused powers* are prior to their action, although *acquired powers* are posterior to their actions, of which they are the result and consequence. It follows that *infused* powers may exist where their action is from circumstances hindered or impossible—and so, that all sacraments in which there is not required an act or acts on the part of the receiver, but in which there is a spiritual *power* divinely given, may be received by children and others who lack the use of reason. This, however, with a distinction. In order to the reception of minor orders there are required years, by reason of the dignity of the sacrament, but not necessarily either of precept or as of necessity to the sacrament. But in order to the reception of sacred orders, there is required the use of reason, on account of their dignity; of necessity of precept, in consequence of the vow of continence annexed to them, and because also to them is committed the handling of the sacraments.

CCCLXIX. No man can give to another that which is not his own. So a slave, who has not power over his own body, is not to receive orders, whereby one enters the Divine service. But, nevertheless, should orders be conferred upon him, he truly receives them, because bondage does not hinder the power, but the act only. A slave is not incapacitated by subjection in the same way as a woman, who is subject *by nature*.

CCCLXX. Since homicide is especially repugnant to peace, of which the Eucharist is the Sacrament, homicides are debarred from orders which have the celebration of the Eucharist for their end; but this by precept of the Church—not as of necessity to the Sacrament.

CCCLXXI. In like manner, of precept, although not of sacramental necessity, men illegitimately born are debarred from orders, inasmuch as, the ordained being promoted to a certain dignity above their fellows, their dignity is obscured by a base origin. This impediment may however be dispensed; but the baser the origin the more difficult is it to procure the dispensation.

CCCLXXII. In like manner also, notable defects, such as either, 1, disfigure or deface the person; or. 2, would hinder execution of the functions pertaining to the several orders, debar from their reception.

CCCLXXIII. It is fitting that those who receive the sacred orders should have their hair shorn and shaven, and that in the form of a crown—1, because, as S. Gregory says, To serve God is to reign, and the crown is the sign of reigning or kingship. 2. A crown is the sign of perfection, and the servants of God ought to be perfect in all virtue, and in every good work. 3. Hair is given for a veil or covering, but the ministers of the altar ought to have the veil taken from before their minds. 4. Hair is generated of superfluity, but the ministers of the mysteries ought to put away from them all superfluity.

CCCLXXIV. By the *corona* or tonsure is delivered no special determinate power of order. It is a deputation of the person to those ministries of the Church which are common to the whole college of ministers, such as to sing the Divine praise. The tonsure is not an order; it is a preamble to orders.

It does not imprint *character*, although it has some inward and spiritual effect corresponding to it, as does the signified to the sign. The deputation to the Divine *cultus* which the *corona* signifies and implies, ought to be made by the chief of the ministers, to wit, the Bishop, to whom it also belongs to bless the vestments, the vessels, and all else appertaining thereto.

CCCLXXV. Men who receive the tonsure, so becoming clerks *(clerici)* are not held thereby to renounce their patrimony or other temporal goods, because it is only too great affection for and not the possession of these which is repugnant to or interferes with the Divine *cultus* to which they are then and thereby deputed. Otherwise there would be no difference between religious and secular clerks.

CCCLXXVI. A priest has two acts. 1. One, and that the principal, to consecrate the Body of Christ. 2. The other, and that the secondary, to prepare the people of God for Its reception. As to the first of these acts the power of the priest does not depend on any superior power, save the Divine. As to the second, it depends on a power superior and human. For every power which cannot proceed to and issue in an act, unless certain ordinations be presupposed, depends on that power which makes these ordinations; but a priest cannot absolve or bind unless by a presupposed jurisdiction of prelation whereby those whom he absolves have been made subject to him. But a priest can consecrate any matter which has been determined by Christ, nor is aught else required than such determination as of necessity to the sacrament, although of congruity there are presupposed episcopal acts in the consecration of the altar, the vestments, and the like. It is clear, then, that there ought to be, above the sacerdotal, episcopal power, in order to the secondary act of the priesthood, whereby a priest may receive power to bind and loose, although not in order to the primary and principal act.

The sacerdotal power extends to purging and illuminating; the episcopal adds to these the power of perfecting.

The Divine ministries ought to be better ordained than the human, but the order of human offices exacts that in every office there be set up one who shall be the prince of that office. And so over priests there must needs be set one who shall be prince of the priests, that is, who shall be Bishop.

Like a Bishop, Aaron was both priest and pontiff. As Priest he was not superior to the least in the priesthood who could offer sacrifice as well as he. As Pontiff he excelled them all in that he had functions peculiar to himself, as to enter once in the year into the Holy of Holies, and the like.

CCCLXXVII. As the perfections of all things natural pre-existed *ex emplariter* in God, so was Christ the exemplar of all ecclesiastical offices. Hence every minister of the Church, in some particular, is a type of Christ; yet is he the superior who according to the greatest perfection represents Christ. A Priest represents Christ in this that by Himself He fulfilled a ministry, but a Bishop in this that he instituted other ministers and founded the Church. Hence to a Bishop it belongs to ordain men to ecclesiastical offices, and to order the Divine *cultus* according to the similitude of Christ. Wherefore also the Bishop is in a special manner called the Spouse of the Church *(Sponsus Ecclesiæ)* as was also Christ.

CCCLXXVIII. The Episcopate cannot be called an order, if order be considered as it is a sacrament ordained in order to the Eucharist, with regard to which a Bishop has no more power than a priest; but it may be called an order,.

if order be considered, as it is an office ordained in respect of certain sacred actions. A Bishop has power in hierarchical actions in respect of the Mystical Body above that of a Priest, and in this sense the Episcopate is an order.

The Episcopate does not imprint *character*.

CCCLXXIX. Seeing the whole Church is one body, it is agreeable to right reason that if its unity is to be preserved there must be a governing power in respect of the whole Church above the Episcopal power, whereby every special church is governed; and this is the power of the Pope. Those therefore who deny this power are called Schismaticks, as dividers of the unity of the Church. Between a simple Bishop and the Pope there are also other degrees of dignity corresponding to the degrees of union according to which one congregation or community includes another; as, for instance, the community of a province includes that of a city, and the community of a kingdom includes that of one province, and the community of the whole world includes that of one kingdom.

The Council of Constantinople decreed that, according to the Scriptures and according to the statutes and definitions of the Canons, they venerated the most holy Bishop of Old Rome as the first and greatest *(primus et maximus)* of the Bishops, and after him the Bishop of Constantinople.

S. Cyril of Alexandria says that we the members must abide in union with our head, the apostolick throne of the Roman Pontiffs, from which we should ask what to believe and what we ought to hold, venerating it and asking it for all, since to it alone it belongs to rebuke, to correct, to decree, to set in order, to loose and to bind, in the place of Him who built it up. On it and on none other He bestowed His own fullness; to it all *jure divino* bow the head, and to it the princes of the world yield obedience as to the Lord Jesus Christ Himself.

CCCLXXX. All the Bishops are successors of the Apostles, and the power which was given to one of the Apostles—namely, to S. Peter—was given also to all. But although to all the Apostles was given in common the power of binding and loosing, yet that in this power might be signified a certain order, to S. Peter alone was it given first, and this to show that from him it was to descend to the rest. Wherefore to him it was said in the singular number Strengthen thy brethren, and again, Feed my sheep — that is, as S. Chrysostom says, Be thou in my place head of, and set over thy brethren.

CCCLXXXI. The power of a priest is exceeded by the power of a Bishop as by a power of another *genus;* but the power of a Bishop is exceeded by the power of the Pope as by a power of the same *genus*. Every hierarchical act which the Pope can do in the administration of the sacraments a Bishop can do; but not every act which a Bishop can do is possible to a Priest in the conferring of the sacraments.

Superior power cannot be conferred by inferior, nor can equal by equal, for, as S. Paul teaches, without any contradiction, the less is blessed of the greater; and so one Priest cannot promote another to the Episcopate, neither can he confer the priesthood.

But inasmuch as all Bishops are equal as to those things which are of Episcopal order, one Bishop can consecrate another, and the Bishop of Ostia consecrates the Pope.

CCCLXXXII. The vestments of the ministers signify the worthiness which is required in them in order to the handling of things Divine. Inasmuch as there are some things required of all, and some others required of the superior orders only, and not of the inferior; so are there some vestments common to all, some others reserved to the superior ministers. Common and belonging to all ministers is the *amice*, covering the shoulders, and signifying fortitude in the execution of the Divine offices, to the performance of which they are enlisted. In like manner the *alb*, which signifies purity of life; and the *girdle*, which signifies the keeping under of the flesh. The sub-deacon has besides a *maniple* on his left arm, to signify cleansing from the smallest stains, the maniple being as it were a *sudarium* for wiping the face. Sub-deacons are the lowest admitted to the handling of things sacred. They have also a tight *tunicle*, whereby is signified the doctrine of Christ; hence in the old law there were hung on it bells. They are the lowest admitted to proclaim the doctrine of the New Law. The Deacon has, in addition, a stole over his left shoulder, for a sign that he is bound to minister in the sacraments themselves. He wears also a *dalmatick*, a liberal vestment, and so called because first used in the parts of Dalmatia. It signifies that he is the lowest appointed as a dispenser of the sacraments, for in dispensation is required liberality. To him it belongs to dispense the Blood. The *priest's stole* is placed over both shoulders, to show that to him is given plenary power of dispensing the sacraments, and not as the minister of another, and so the stole descends *usque ad inferiora*. He has also a *chasuble*, which signifies charity, for to him it belongs to consecrate the sacrament of charity—to wit the Eucharist. The Bishops have *nine* ornaments more than the priests. These are—1. boots, 2. sandals, 3. apron, 4. tunic, 5. dalmatick, 6. mitre, 7. gloves, 8. ring, and 9. staff. These correspond to the *nine* functions which are theirs over and above those of the priests, viz.:—1. to ordain clerks, 2. to bless virgins, 3. to consecrate pontiffs, 4. to lay on hands, 5. to dedicate basilicas, 6. to depose clerks, 7. to celebrate Synods, 8. to confect chrism, 9. to hallow vestments and vessels.

1. By the boots is signified the uprightness of his walk ; 2. by the sandals, his contempt of things earthly ; 3. by the apron, whereby the stole is bound with the alb, love of the honourable ; 4. by the tunic, perseverance ; 5. by the dalmatick, liberality in works of mercy ; 6. by the gloves, caution in operation ; 7. by the mitre, knowledge of both testaments—hence its two horns ; 8. by the staff, pastoral care, which ought to gather together the erring, signified by the curved head ; to sustain the infirm, signified by the body of the staff ; and to stir up the lazy, signified by the goad at the end, as indicated in the verse:

Collige, sustenta, stimula, vaga, morbida, lenta.

9. The ring signifies the sacraments of the faith, whereby the Church is espoused to Christ, for the Bishops, as His vicars, are the spouses of the Church. In token of their power of privilege Archbishops wear the *pallium*.

8. THE SACRAMENT OF MATRIMONY.

CCCLXXXIII. MATRIMONY is said to be of the law of nature, or natural. 1. By reason of its principal final cause, which is offspring. For nature intends not only the generation of offspring, but their upbringing and arrival at man's estate; as the Philosopher says, we have three things from our parents, viz., being, nurture, and discipline. Now a son cannot be educated and instructed by his parents, unless it be determined and certain that he has parents, which it would not be unless there were a certain determinate obligation of a man to a woman—which makes matrimony. 2. By reason of its secondary end, which is the mutual accommodation of the spouses to each other in matters domestic. For as natural reason dictates that men should live together, whence man is said to be naturally political; and seeing that certain necessary works pertain rather to the man, and certain others to the woman, nature prompts an association of a man with a woman, wherein consists Matrimony. Matrimony is then a necessary consequence of man's being naturally political, gregal, and conjugal.

CCCLXXXIV. Procreation of offspring is common to all animals; but the offspring of some animals can as soon as born get their own living: in this case, there is no determination of the male to the female. The same holds good when sustentation is required on the part of the mother only. The offspring of others requires the sustentation of both parents, but for a short time, and here there is found a determination of the male to the female for that time, as in the case of certain birds. But human offspring requires parental care for a long time, and so between man and woman there is the greatest determination.

CCCLXXXV. Cicero indeed says that in the beginning men were savages, having no fixed wives, and knowing not their own children, but he is speaking of the beginning of certain distinct peoples; and Holy Scripture relates that from the beginning of the human race there existed wedlock.

CCCLXXXVI. Men are not bound by precept to contract matrimony, since it is a hindrance to the contemplative life, which it is for the perfection of mankind at large that some should embrace. This was allowed even by the ancient philosophers. Theophrastus proves that for a *savant* it is not expedient to marry.

CCCLXXXVII. The precept to increase and multiply no more obliges every man than the precept to till the ground. S. Paul writes to the Corinthians, that he that joineth not his virgin in matrimony doth better than he that doth so join her. And so matrimony cannot be of precept. Neither can that be of precept, abstinence from which is rewarded. But to virgins is promised the special reward of the *aureola*.

CCCLXXXVIII. Since matrimony itself was instituted for the procreation of offspring, the act thereof is always lawful, and also meritorious, if an act of justice, or a payment of debt demanded, or an act of religion, in order to the procreation of worshippers of God; otherwise the act is a venial sin.

So much for matrimony as an office of Nature.

CCCLXXXIX. Matrimony is a sacrament, since it exhibits to man a remedy of sanctity against sin.

CCCXC. The words which express the matrimonial consent are the *form* of this sacrament, and not the benediction of the priest, which is only *quoddam sacramentale*.

CCCXCI. In Matrimony, as in Penance, the *matter* of the Sacrament is the act of him who uses it.

CCCXCII. True sacraments have efficacy from the Passion of Christ, to which men are by them conformed. And although by Matrimony a man is not conformed to the Passion of Christ as regards its pain, yet he is as regards its charity, by reason of which Christ suffered for the Church, which is His Bride. S. Paul, writing to the Ephesians, says, This is a great Sacrament.

CCCXCIII. Matrimony, as an Office of Nature, ordained for the procreation of offspring, which was necessary before the existence of sin, was instituted in the Estate of Innocence. As it is a remedy against the wound of sin, it was instituted after the fall, and under the Law of Nature. As to determination of persons, it had institution in the Law of Moses. But as representing the mysterious union between Christ and His Church, it was instituted under the New Law, and, according to this, is a Sacrament of the New Law; with regard to its other ends, a friendship and the mutual service of the spouses, it has institution in the Civil Law.

Matrimony before sin was instituted by God, when having from the rib of the man formed the woman, He said to both, Increase and multiply.

CCCXCIV. Matrimony, contracted in the faith of Christ, confers grace, aiding a man in the performance of those things which are thereby required. Whenever there is a faculty divinely given, there are given aids in order that it may be properly used. All the powers of the soul have some corresponding members of the body, by means of which they may proceed to action.

Were matrimony only a sign, and not a cause of grace, it would in no way excel the Sacraments of the Old Law.

CCCXCV. Matrimony is perfect and complete as to its essence, *sine copulâ*, but not as to its operation or use. Copulation is not of the integrity of matrimony, for in Paradise, before the fall, there was matrimony, but no copulation.

CCCXCVI. Consent to conjugal copulation by words *de futuro* does not make matrimony, but a promise of matrimony; and this promise is called Espousals. This promise may be made, 1. either absolutely, or 2. conditionally. If absolutely, in four ways, 1. by a bare promise, as, when it is said, I will take you for mine; 2. when an earnest is given, as money or the like; 3. by the giving of a ring; 4. by the intervention of an oath. If conditionally, 1. the condition may be honourable, as, I will take you, if it please my parents, and then, if the condition stand, the promise stands—if the condition fall, the promise falls; or, 2. the condition may be dishonourable, and this, either contrary to the good of matrimony, as, I will take you, if you will procure sterility; and then no espousals are contracted: or, not contrary thereto, as, I will take you, if you will consent to my thefts; in which case the promise stands, but the condition is to be abrogated.

CCCXCVII. An espoused person who does not fulfil his or her promise sins mortally, unless there have intervened a lawful impediment. But although the Church will put such an one to penance for the sin, yet, in consideration of the evil results of forced marriages, he will not be compelled to matrimony.

CCCXCVIII. A condition, which is a promise under a penalty, and not a mere promise of dowry, will not stand, nor can the penalty be exacted from him or her who will not complete the matrimony.

CCCXCIX. A man may at the end of his first seven years contract espousals; 2. at the end of his second seven years dispose of his body either by, i. contracting marriage, or, ii. entering religion; 3. at the end of his third seven years he may bind himself by civil contracts, and dispose of his substance.

CCCC. If a contract of espousal have been made by a third party for spouses beneath the years of puberty, one or both may reclaim; and in this case no affinity has been contracted. If, on arriving at due age, they do not reclaim, they are understood to consent to the arrangements made by others for them.

CCCCI. The same age, seven years, the earliest limit of espousals, is fixed for both boys and girls, because both attain the use of reason at the same time. But for contracting matrimony there is required a disposition not only of mind but of body, in regard of which fourteen years is fixed as the earliest limit for a boy, and twelve for a girl.

CCCCII. Espousals are *ipso jure* sundered, 1. when either of the spouses enters religion, or, 2. contracts matrimony with another by words *de praesenti*. In all other cases they are sundered only by sentence of the Church.

CCCCIII. If, before contracting matrimony, either of the spouses fall victim to a grievous infirmity which, 1. greatly debilitates, as epilepsy, or paralysis; or, 2. deforms, as loss of the nose or of an eye; or, 3. would infect offspring, as leprosy, their espousals may be sundered, lest these infirmities should engender dislikes, and their matrimony produce evil results.

CCCCIV. As affinity, if it had been contracted at the time of the espousals, would have hindered the contract, so if it intervene between them and the matrimony which is their effect, the contract is hindered from being fulfilled. This affinity might be contracted by the fornication of the one spouse with the blood relation of the other who, in this case, would lose nothing, but rather gain by being loosed from him who by fornication had made himself hateful to God.

CCCCV. Matrimony is an ordination of two persons, a conjunction of a man and a woman, who therein become husband and wife in order to the generation and education of one offspring, and the leading of one domestic life.

CCCCVI. In matrimony three things have to be considered—1. its essence, which is union, and by reason of this it is called wedlock *(conjugium)*; 2. its cause, which is desponsation, and by reason of this it is called nuptials, from the veiling of the woman; 3. its effect, which is offspring, and by reason of this it is called also matrimony. It is so called either—1. As S. Augustine says, because a woman ought not to be veiled save in order that she may be a mother; or, 2. as *matris munium*, because the office of educating the offspring is incumbent chiefly on the woman; or, 3, as *matrem muniens*, because she thereby obtains a defender in the man; or, 4. as *matrem monens*, admonishing her to cleave to her husband; or, 5. as *materia unius*, the union contributing the joint matter of the one offspring (μονος); or, 6. as Isidore says, because a woman thereby becomes *mater nati*.

CCCCVII. Matrimony is an indissoluble—marital—union between legitimate persons, maintaining an undivided habit of life.

CCCCVIII. In all sacraments there is spiritual operation through the means of *(mediante)* material operation, which also signifies it: as by corporal ablution in Baptism there is effected interior spiritual ablution. And hence, since in Matrimony there is spiritual union, in as much as Matrimony is a Sacrament, and also material union according as it is for an office of nature and of civil life, the spiritual union which is effected by divine virtue, must needs be *mediante* the material. Now the unions of material contracts are made by mutual consent; and so in like manner by mutual consent is the matrimonial union effected.

CCCCIX. The first cause of the Sacraments is divine virtue, which in and by them works salvation. But the second or instrumental causes are material operations, which have their efficacy of divine institution: And it is in this way that consent is the cause in Matrimony.

CCCCX. To every sacrament there must be a sensible sign, and so in the Sacrament of Matrimony there is the sensible sign of the words which express the consent.

CCCCXI. As in all other material contracts so also in the matrimonial union of man and woman, their consent must be expressed by words.

CCCCXII. True, a vow obliges *quoad* God, even although not expressed in words, but then, be it remembered, there is in a vow no sacramental obligation, but spiritual obligation only.

CCCCXIII. Signs, as a nod, take the place of, and are counted as words, when, as in the case of dumb persons, or persons of different languages, words are impossible.

CCCCXIV. The words of parents are reckoned as those of the damsel their daughter, unless they are contradicted by her.

CCCCXV. Sacramental causes effect while they signify, and so effect what they signify. But if a man express his consent by words *de futuro*, he does not thereby signify that he makes matrimony, but promises that he will make it. Such an expression of consent therefore, by words *de futuro*, does not make matrimony, but a promise of it, or, in other words, Espousals. The use of future words in contracts does not transfer power over anything from one's self to another. I will give you is not synonymous with I give. To take an instance. If a man consents to matrimony with one woman by words *de futuro*, and thereafter with another by words *de præsenti*, he has sinned mortally by breaking his promise or oath, as the case may be, to the first, but he is *married* to the second.

CCCCXVI. Consent expressed by exterior words without interior consent does not make matrimony, any more than exterior ablution makes Baptism, when, through jest or deceit, there is no interior intention to receive that Sacrament.

CCCCXVII. If there be wanting mental consent on the part of one, there is matrimony on the part of neither, because matrimony consists in mutual union. But it may be probably believed that there is no fraud, unless evident signs thereof be apparent, because good is to be presumed of every one whomsoever until the contrary be proved. The party on whose side there is no fraud is by ignorance excused from sin.

CCCCXVIII. Supposing a man is proved to have consented by words *de præsenti* to one woman, he is compelled under pain of excommunication to have her to wife, even although he declare that mental consent was wanting, nay even although he have afterwards contracted with another with mental consent expressed in words *de præsenti;* and, in so judging, the Church which judges according to what is outwardly apparent, is not deceived either in justice or in law, but in fact only. But the man ought rather to bear the excommunication than to approach his first wife, or he ought to fly to remote regions.

CCCCXIX. Secret consent expressed by words *de præsenti* between persons who may lawfully contract, although wicked and contrary to law, does yet make matrimony, as comprehending its essence, although not the solemnities with which it is ordinarily and meetly surrounded. Although their matrimony is valid, yet they sin who so contract it, unless excused for some lawful cause.

CCCCXX. A damsel is not in the power of her father as a slave, so that she may not have power over her own body, but as a daughter, to educate; and therefore, so she be a free woman, she may give herself into the power of another without her father's consent ; even as without consent of parents any man or woman may enter religion, so that they be free persons.

CCCCXXI. Consent expressed by words *de futuro* does not effect matrimony, even although confirmed by an oath, which only confirms what is signified by the words said, and does not alter their signification, or change the future into the present.

CCCCXXII. Copula following on espousals is held *in foro Ecclesiæ* as signifying consent to effect matrimony, unless evident sign of guile or fraud be apparent ; but not *in foro conscientiæ*, if mental consent have been wanting.

CCCCXXIII. If a woman admit her spouse, believing that he wishes to consummate their matrimony, she is excused from sin, unless there be any evident sign of fraud, as would be likely in the case of any great discrepancy of rank or fortune. The man commits fornication, and is to be punished for fraud.

CCCCXXIV. There is a difference between coaction and violence. *Violence* causes a thing to be done of *absolute necessity*, as when one corporally impels another to motion. *Coaction*, or as the Philosopher calls it, *mixed violence*, causes a thing to be *done of conditional necessity*, that is by reason of circumstances. As, for instance, by reason of imminent peril. Now, although there cannot be in matrimony a coacted consent *simpliciter*, or violence, yet there may be a certain violence, *secundum quid*, that is relatively, or by reason of circumstances.

CCCCXXV. A man is compelled by fear, when he does something which he would otherwise not do, in order to avoid that which he fears. Now, there are three sorts of men : a constant man, an inconstant man, and a pertinacious man. A constant man is governed by right reason, and may be compelled to endure a less evil for the sake of avoiding a greater, but is never compelled to a greater evil in order to avoid a less. This an inconstant man is compelled to, as for instance, to sin by the fear of bodily punishment. A pertinacious man, on the other hand, cannot be compelled even to endure or do a less evil in order to avoid a greater. A constant man stands, therefore, midway between an inconstant man and a pertinacious man : he fears but does not fear what, where and when he ought not. Sins being of all the evils the greatest, a constant man cannot be compelled to them; nay, he ought rather to die than do them; but there are certain bodily evils worse than others, as death, blows, imprisonment, rape, bondage, as in the verse:

Stupri sive status, verberis atque necis.

And it matters not whether the injuries be inflicted on one's own person or on the person of one's wife or children.

Such a coaction by fear as occurs in the case of a constant man, hinders consent and so destroys matrimony, which signifies the union of Christ with the Church, which is according to the liberty of love.

CCCCXXVII. Matrimony denoting the *mutual* relation and union of two persons, consent being compelled *ex parte* of either, there is matrimony *ex parte* of neither. A man cannot be the husband of her who (from compelled consent) is not his wife, and similarly a woman cannot be the wife of him who, for the like reason, is not her husband. If there be an impediment on the part of the one, there is no matrimony on the part of the other.

Even the relation of friendship requires the mutual consent of two persons.

CCCCXXVII. Conditional consent *de præsenti*, the condition not being contrary to the goods of matrimony, and conditional consent *de futuro*, the condition being necessary, effect matrimony, in like manner as stated above in the case of espousals. A necessary condition is reckoned as present, the future being present in its cause. But a contingent condition, as the obtaining of a dowry or parental consent, is the same as a consent by words *de futuro*, and so does not make matrimony.

CCCCXXVIII. Since by matrimony a man is bound to a perpetual servitude, a father cannot compel his son to marry of precept, although he may urge him to do so of a reasonable cause; but the precept is binding in proportion as the cause is reasonable.

CCCCXXIX. The consent which makes matrimony is a consent to matrimony, as the proper effect of the will is the thing willed. Therefore as copula stands to matrimony, so does the consent which causes matrimony stand to copula. Now, matrimony, as above shewn, does not consist *essentially* in carnal union, but is an association of a man and a woman *in order thereto*, and to those things thereto appertaining in respect thereof. This association is called conjugal copula, and they have spoken well who have said that to consent to matrimony is to consent to cupola *implicitly*, but not *explicitly*; for it ought not to be understood save as the effect is *implicitly* contained in its cause, and the power of copula to which parties consent is the cause of copula, as the power of using a thing is the cause of its use.

CCCCXXX. Matrimony begun corresponds to matrimony consummated, as does the habit or power to the act which is its operation.

CCCCXXXI. Matrimony contracted for a dishonourable cause is yet true matrimony, although the cause of consent be blameworthy. The first final cause of matrimony, namely, the procreation of offspring and avoidance of fornication, is always good; but its secondary or accidental causes, infinite possibly in number, are good or evil as the case may be.

CCCCXXXII. No wise man ought to suffer loss, save for a recompensation of something equal to or better than the thing lost, and so that which has loss annexed to it ought to have annexed to it also some *good* by way of compensation. Now in the union of man and woman there occurs a loss of reason, on account of the vehemence of the delectation which absorbs it, and there is also tribulation of the flesh and solicitude about things temporal; and so by way of recompensation there must be some goods which excuse matrimony, and render it honourable.

Again, matrimony is an indulgence to man's infirmity, and every indulgence requires a compensating good by way of excuse.

CCCCXXXIII. The three goods of matrimony are—1. Offspring: 2. Fidelity; and 3. Sacramentality. The first two belong to it as it is ordained for an office of nature; the third as it is also a sacrament.

CCCCXXXIV. Of these three goods sacramentality is the principal if we look to order of dignity, inasmuch as the perfection of grace excels the perfection of nature; but *essentially*, intention of offspring has the first place, then fidelity, and lastly sacramentality.

CCCCXXXV. The bond of matrimony does not extend beyond the present life, in which it is contracted, for in the resurrection they neither marry nor are given in marriage. It is said to be inseparable because it cannot be separated in this life but by death—either corporal death after carnal union, or spiritual death after spiritual union only.

CCCCXXXVI. Although the act of matrimony may appear but little honourable on account of the unbridled delectation which always accompanies it, yet its three goods—Offspring, Fidelity, and Sacramentality, not only excuse it, but even render it holy.

CCCCXXXVII. A man by the act of matrimony does not incur the loss of reason as a habit, but only as an act. And sometimes a good act may be interrupted and give place to one less good, without sin, as when one ceases from an act of contemplation in order to give himself to action.

CCCCXXXVIII. The matrimonial act is always culpable and a sin, at least a venial sin, unless there be on the part of the wedded intention of procreating offspring, or of paying the marriage debt, payment of which is included in the good of Fidelity.

Avoidance of fornication, or acquirement or preservation of health, do not remove it from the category of at least venial sins. In the one case it is an indulgence, in the other a means not ordained to that end.

If, however, there be sought a delectation beyond the limits of honourable matrimony, as if a man regard his wife, not as his wife, but simply as a woman, and be ready to do the same with her, were she not his wife, it is a mortal sin. Such an one is called *ardentior amator uxoris*.

CCCCXXXIX. In matrimony there are certain things which are of its essence, and certain which only add to its solemnity, as in other sacraments. In it, as in them, those things being taken away which pertain merely to solemnity, it yet remains a true sacrament. The impediments, therefore, which are contrary to its solemnity merely, do not hinder it from being true matrimony. Such are said to impede the contracting of matrimony, but not to destroy it when contracted, *e.g.*, the prohibition of the Church, and forbidden times, as in the verses—

> Ecclesiae vetitum, necnon tempus feriatum,
> Impediunt fieri, permittunt juncta teneri.

But the impediments which are contrary to those things which are of the essence of matrimony, cause it not to be true matrimony, and so are said not only to impede the contracting, but also to destroy it when contracted, as in the verses—

> Error, conditio, votum, cognatio, crimen,
> Cultus disparitas, vis, ordo, ligamen, honestas,
> Si sis affinis, si forte coire nequibis,
> Haec socianda vetant connubia, facta retractant.

To explain: Matrimony may be impeded either *ex parte* of the contract, or *ex parte* of the contractors. If in the first mode, the voluntary consent which makes matrimony may be destroyed by ignorance or by violence. This supplies two impediments, viz., 1. *compulsion* (vis), and 2. *error*. In the second mode, matrimony may be impeded *ex parte* of the contractors, and that either *simpliciter*, or with respect to others. If *simpliciter* either by 3. *impotence*, or, 4. by want of freedom, *conditio servitutis*. These are impediments *de facto;* they may exist also *de jure*, as in the case of an obligation to continence, whether undertaken by the reception of an office or by the making of a vow. This gives 5 and 6, order and vow. With respect to others, 7. previous matrimony is an impediment; also 8. difference of religion; 9. cognation; 10. affinity by marriage; 11. affinity by espousal, and 12. previous adultery of the parties.

CCCCXL. Since error hinders consent, which is the efficient cause of matrimony, it hinders also, and that by the law of nature, matrimony, which is its effect.

But the error must concern those things which are of the essence of matrimony, as, 1. an error of person; or, 2. an error of condition, as in the case of a slave who cannot transfer to another that power over his body which he does not himself possess. No error as to fortune, or nobility, or quality of body or mind is an impediment, unless it can be comprehended under one or other of those two.

CCCCXLI. Matrimony is of the law of Nature; bondage is of positive law. But that which is of the positive law cannot prejudice that which is of the law of Nature, and so a slave may, without the knowledge or consent, and even against the will of his lord, freely contract matrimony, as he may freely eat or sleep, or do aught else which Nature ordains in order to the preservation of his body or species. The servant is bound to obey his lord in those things only which pertain to lordship.

A slave may vow continence without the consent of his lord.

Matrimony is contracted in the faith of Christ Jesus, and in Him there is neither bond nor free.

CCCCXLII. A man being by matrimony subjected to his wife, as to natural acts only, to which bondage does not extend, he may, without the consent of his wife, yield himself for a slave, and the matrimony is not thereby dissolved—which, indeed, it cannot be by any *supervening* impediment.

CCCCXLIII. Since the condition of bondage attaches itself to the corporal substance which is derived from the mother, the father supplying its formal complement, the offspring reasonably follows the mother rather than the father as to condition, whether of freedom or bondage: and this according both to the Canon Law and the Law of Moses. But in some countries which are not ruled by the Canon Law, the offspring takes the condition of the inferior parent.

If one man sows in another man's land, the fruits are his to whom the land belongs.

Animals begotten of diverse species resemble the mother rather than the father. Thus a mule born of a mare and an ass resembles a horse more than an ass; while one born of a horse and a she-ass resembles the latter more than the former.

CCCCXLIV. A *simple vow* of continence hinders the contracting of matrimony, but does not destroy it when contracted. A simple vow is a promise, not a transference of one's dominion over one's body. He who transfers it to a wife sins by breaking his promise; but the transference is valid, and in it consists matrimony, which is indissoluble. He who contracts matrimony by words *de præsenti* after a simple vow, cannot consummate it without mortal sin. After its consummation he is bound to pay, but is not entitled to demand the marriage debt.

CCCCXLV. He who makes a *solemn vow* contracts spiritual matrimony with God, which is of greater dignity than material matrimony. But even a previous material matrimony not only prevents the contracting of subsequent matrimony, but destroys the contract, much more spiritual matrimony, whereby a man loses and transfers his power over his own body.

CCCCXLVI. The Priesthood among the Greeks and other Easterns impedes the contracting of matrimony, but not the use of matrimony previously contracted. This it does with them *ex vi ordinis*, but in the Western Church not only *ex vi ordinis*, but *ex vi* also of the vow of continence annexed to the subdiaconate and other higher orders. Holy Orders not only impede the contracting, but destroy the contract.

It is but congruous and becoming that those who, being in Holy Orders, have to handle the sacred vessels and sacraments, should by continence preserve corporal purity.

CCCCXLVII. Matrimony does not impede the reception of Holy Orders. A man may present himself without the consent, and even against the will of his wife, and he receives the *character* of order, albeit he is deprived of its *execution*. But if she be dead, or have given her consent, he receives both.

As a man may after matrimony yield himself a slave to his fellow-man, so may he also yield himself a servant to God, either in Orders or in religion.

CCCCXLVIII. Consanguinity is the bond contracted by carnal propagation between those who descend from the same stock.

CCCCXLIX. The degrees or lines of Consanguinity are—1. The descending from one common stock; 2. The ascending thereto; 3. The transversal.

CCCCL. To know the degree of Consanguinity in which one person is distant from another, the following rules are to be observed:—First, in the direct line ascending or descending, as many degrees are to be numbered as persons, except the first; therefore the son is in the first degree of consanguinity with the father, the grandson in the second, the great grandson in the third, and so on. Secondly, in the cross line, when two parties are equally distant from the original stock, by how many degrees they are distant from it, so many exactly are they distant from each other. Hence brothers and sisters are in the first degree of consanguinity with each other, because they are in the first degree of consanguinity with the father, and their children are in the second degree with each other for the same reason. Thirdly, in the collateral line, when two persons are not equally distant from the common stock, by how many degrees the more remote party is distant from the original stock, so many exactly is he distant from the other. Hence the son of the brother is distant from his uncle in the second degree, because he is distant from his grandfather in that degree.

CCCCLI. In matrimony that is said to be against the law of nature, whereby matrimony is rendered incompetent in respect of the end to which it has been ordained. This end *per se* and primarily is the Good of offspring, and by certain consanguinities, as those between father and daughter and mother and son, it is impeded, albeit not wholly destroyed, because the daughter can conceive offspring of the seed of her father, and along with him nourish and instruct them, wherein consists the Good of offspring. But it is far from fitting, for it is inordinate that a daughter be joined to her father by matrimony for a consort or partner *(socia)* in order to beget and educate offspring, who should in all things be subject to her father, as having proceeded from him. And so it is of the natural law that father and mother be excluded from matrimony; and the mother even more than the father, because it derogates more from that reverence which is due to parents if the son marry the mother than if the father marry the daughter, since the wife must be subject to the husband.

But a secondary end of matrimony is the repression of concupiscence; and this would be undone if one might marry one's relative by consanguinity, for a great door would be opened to concupiscence unless carnal union were forbidden between certain persons who ought of necessity to live together beneath the same roof. By the divine law, therefore, such persons are excluded from matrimony.

Further, an accidental end of matrimony is the confederation of men, and the multiplication of amities, in that the man stands in the same relation to his wife's relatives by consanguinity, as to his own. This confederation would be prejudiced were a man to take a wife of his own blood, thus introducing no new bond of society. Both by human and by ecclesiastical laws, therefore, other and more remote degrees of consanguinity are excluded from matrimony. It may be said then, 1, that consanguinity impedes matrimony between certain persons of the *natural law;* between certain others of the *divine law;* and certain more of *human laws.*

CCCCLII. At divers times, to meet their diverse necessities, diverse degrees of consanguinity have been prohibited from matrimony. In the beginning of the human race, by reason of the fewness of mankind, only the father and the mother were prohibited. In the law of Moses were prohibited those persons who were wont to live together, as was meet, beneath the same roof. But the Old Law permitted, nay prescribed, matrimony within certain degrees of consanguinity, in order to prevent confusion in the succession to inheritances, and to provide for the due worship of God by a succession of worshippers. But afterwards by the New Law, which is the law of the Spirit and of love, more grades of consanguinity were prohibited, because then by spiritual grace and not by carnal origin the worship of God was derived and multiplied, and because it was meet that men should then be more withdrawn from carnal matters, and more given to spiritual, in order that love might more abound. By reason of this matrimony was anciently forbidden even to the seventh degree, as well because beyond it the memory of a common root would not easily remain, as having reference also to the septiform grace of the Holy Ghost. But in these last times the interdict of the Church has been restricted to the fourth degree. 1. Because there is between more remote degrees no closer bond of amity than between extraneous persons; and, 2, lest the prohibition of so many degrees should by reason of men's lust and negligence become to them for a snare.

The prohibition is very fittingly restricted to the fourth degree, because to the fourth generation men are wont to survive, and so the memory of their consanguinity is not likely to be lost; hence it is that God threatens to visit the sins of the parents on the children to the third and fourth generations; 2, because in every generation there is a new mixture of foreign blood. Identity of blood makes consanguinity; and in proportion to the accession of fresh blood, is the loss of identity with the original. It is such after the fourth generation that carnal union may be reiterated.

CCCCLIII. Affinity is a relationship between two persons, arising from a carnal union of one person with the blood relation of the other. To understand the different degrees of affinity, the following rule is to be observed: Suppose a marriage contracted between two parties, in whatever degree a person is connected by consanguinity with the man, in the same degree is he connected by affinity with the woman. But although all those related by consanguinity with the man contract an affinity with his wife; and, on the other hand, all the blood relations of the wife contract an affinity with the husband, nevertheless the blood relations of the wife and the husband do not contract an affinity with each other.

CCCCLIV. The affinity of two persons is not destroyed by the death of the third party, by reason of whose consanguinity it was contracted.

CCCCLV. Affinity, being caused by carnal union, proceeds from fornication as well as from matrimony, carnal union being common to both.

CCCCLVI. Since espousals are not matrimony, but only preparatory thereto, being an agreement and promise of future conjugal society, affinity is not contracted by them, although there arises from them something resembling affinity, called the Justice of the Public Honour, which impedes matrimony as do consanguinity and affinity, and in the same degree. It derives its strength from the Church's institution, and is ordained with a view to the public expediency.

CCCCLVII. Affinity does not cause affinity.

CCCCLVIII. There being a necessity for friendship and cohabitation in the case of relations by affinity, as in the case of relations by consanguinity, affinity preceding matrimony not only hinders the contracting thereof, but destroys it when contracted. See No. CCCCLI.
This supervening affinity cannot do.

CCCCLIX. Distinction of degrees *per se* belongs to consanguinity, and not to affinity, save *mediante consanguinitate*. The general rule to find the degrees of affinity is, In whatsoever degree of consanguinity the man is related to me, in the same degree of affinity is related his wife.
This being so, there are as many degrees of affinity as there are degrees of consanguinity; but inasmuch as the bond of affinity is less strict than that of consanguinity, so, both in the old times and now, a dispensation is more easily obtained in the remote degrees of affinity than in the remote degrees of consanguinity.

CCCCLX. In the Jewish law, a man, on the death of his brother, leaving a widow without offspring, was to take his brother's wife, his own sister by affinity, and raise up seed unto his brother; but only in this case, and for this end. It was requisite at that time, when the number of the worshippers of God, of the true religion was multiplied by the process of carnal propagation, which is not now the case. Moreover, the man did not take his sister-in-law to wife *in his own person*, but in order to supply the defect of his brother.

CCCCLXI. As carnal cognation both impedes the contracting of matrimony and destroys it when contracted, so does also spiritual cognation, preceding the matrimony: this it does of ecclesiastical ordinance.

CCCCLXII. By two sacraments—namely by Baptism and Confirmation, is spiritual cognation contracted, inasmuch as both have relation to spiritual nativity or regeneration. Carnal nativity is twofold. First in the womb, in which that which is borne is yet debile, and cannot, without peril, be exposed. To this nativity is assimilated regeneration by baptism, in which one is regenerated, but to be cherished for a season within the womb of the Church. The second nativity is from the womb, when that which has been borne therein has become so strengthened that it may, without peril, be exposed. To this is assimilated confirmation, whereby a man is strengthened before being exposed to the publick confession of the faith of Christ.

As by espousals, which are a promise of future nuptials, so by catechism, which is a profession of future baptism, there is contracted, not a real, but a kind of propinquity, called a *debile impedimentum*, which does not destroy the contract, but hinders the contracting of marriage.

CCCCLXIII. As in carnal generation one is born of father and mother, so in spiritual regeneration one is reborn the son of God, as his Father, and the son of the Church as his Mother. Now as he who confers the sacrament, personates God, whose instrument and minister he is; so he or she who receives the baptized from the sacred font, or holds him to be confirmed, personates the Church. In both cases there is contracted spiritual cognation.

CCCCLXIV. Spiritual cognation passes from a man to the wife, or woman whom he has carnally known. It passes also to the carnal sons of a spiritual father.

There are three spiritual cognations. 1. *Spiritual paternity*, which is the relation between the spiritual father and the spiritual son. 2. *Compaternity*, which is the relation between the spiritual father and the carnal father of the same son. 3. *Spiritual fraternity*, which is the relation between the spiritual son and the carnal sons of the same father.

Each of these spiritual cognations both hinders the contracting of matrimony and destroys it when contracted.

CCCCLXV. Art imitates Nature, and supplies the defects of Nature in those things in which Nature fails. Positive Law, which is the art of Equity, supplies the natural defects of sons by the lawful assumption of extraneous persons to be sons or nephews.

This definition comprehends the *genus* of adoption in the words, *The lawful assumption;* the *terminus a quo—of extraneous persons;* and the *terminus ad quem—to be sons or nephews.*

There are two kinds of adoption. Of these one perfectly imitates natural filiation, and is called *arrogation*. By it the adopted succeeds to the adopting father, if the latter be intestate; nor can the adopting father *sine culpâ* deprive the adopted son of a fourth part of his heritage. But no one can be so adopted unless he have power over himself, unless, that is to say, he have not a father, or, having a father, have been emancipated. In order to it, there must also be interposed the royal authority. 2. The other adoption, which but imperfectly imitates natural filiation, is called *simple adoption*. One may be adopted by simple adoption who is not *sui juris*, and by mere authority of the magistrate, without interposition of the royal authority. But such an one so adopted does not succeed to the goods of his intestate adopter, nor is he bound to leave him anything in his testament unless he so wills.

CCCCLXVI. The Divine Law chiefly excludes from matrimony such persons as it is necessary should cohabit, lest, as the Rabbi Moyses says, if carnal union were allowed to them, an easy door should be opened to concupiscence, which matrimony has been ordained to repress. Now, in as much as an adopted son cohabits with the members of the household of his adopting father, as does a son by nature, it has been decreed by human laws, which have been approved by the Church, that *legal cognation*, which is the propuinquity arising from adoption, is a bar to matrimony.

CCCCLXVII. Legal cognation is threefold, 1. of descendants. This is contracted between an adopting father and an adopted son, and the son of an adoptive son, and the like. 2. The relation between an adoptive son and a son by nature. 3. By way of an affinity, the relation which is between the adopting father, and the wife of the adoptive son, or *e contrario*, between the adopted son and the wife of the adopting father. The first and third of these cognations are perpetual impediments to matrimony; but the second only so long as the son remains under the power of the father adopting; the impediment ceases on the death of the father or the emancipation of the son.

CCCCLXVIII. In matrimony there is a contract whereby each binds himself to the other to pay the marriage debt. As in other contracts, so in this, the parties must be able to give or do that to which they bind themselves; otherwise the contract is null and void. If either party cannot pay the carnal debt, this inability forms an impediment which is called by the general name of *impotence*. Impotence may arise, 1. either from an intrinsic and natural cause; or, 2. from an extrinsic and accidental cause. If from a natural cause, that cause may be twofold, either, 1. temporary, to be removed by medicinal remedies or by advancing years, and, if so, it does not dissolve the matrimony; or, 2. it is perpetual, and then it dissolves the matrimony, so that the one on whose part the impediment is alleged must perpetually remain without hopes of wedlock; the other may marry whom he will, in the Lord. To ascertain whether the impediment be perpetual or not, the Church hath determined a period of experience, to wit, three years. If during that time the parties, having faithfully endeavoured, have failed to consummate their matrimony, it will be dissolved by her decree. But if the Church find that the three years have not been sufficient to prove their impotence, and that she has erred and been deceived thereanent by the subsequent *copula* of the supposed impotent man with another or the same woman, she reintegrates the previous matrimony, and annuls the second matrimony, if such there be.

The same general rules apply in the case of impotence through the agency of evil spirits, as in the case of impotence through frigidity.

CCCCLXIX. Since from the incest, whereby a man knows the sister, or other relation by consanguinity, of his wife, there is contracted an affinity, the contracting of matrimony is thereby impeded, even after espousal. But if the incest have taken place after the matrimony has been contracted and consummated, it is not to be wholly set aside. The man loses the right of demanding the marriage debt, nor can he demand it without sin. But he is nevertheless to pay the debt when demanded by his wife, seeing she ought not to be punished for his sin. After the wife's death the man ought to remain wholly without hope of wedlock, unless he obtain a dispensation by reason of his frailty, and to avoid peril of fornication. If, nevertheless, without a dispensation, he contract matrimony, he sins, doing contrary to the ordinance of the Church; yet is not on this account his matrimony to be set aside. This incest is an impediment to matrimony, not by reason of its guilt, but by reason of the affinity which it causes. It is not therefore reckoned as a separate impediment, but is included under the general impediment of affinity.

CCCCLXX. Since matrimony is made by way of contract, it is subject to the ordinations of positive law, as are other contracts. The law has determined that matrimony be not contracted before that period of discretion at which both parties can sufficiently deliberate as to their choice, and be severally able to pay each to the other the mutual marriage debt. If this ordinance be transgressed, the matrimony is dissolved. This period occurs, for the most part, in men, at their fourteenth year; in women, at their twelfth. Now, the precepts of positive law, in so determining, follow the average. But if any one arrive at the due perfection before the period foresaid, so that the vigour of nature and reason supply the defect of age, their matrimony is not to be dissolved, but remains perpetually indissoluble.

CCCCLXXI. Madness may either precede matrimony or follow it. If it follow it, it in no way destroys it. If it precede it, then the madman either has had lucid intervals, or he has not. If he has, then, although the matrimony which he then contracts be not complete, inasmuch as he knows not how to educate his offspring, yet *it is* matrimony. But if he have no lucid intervals, or if, not during a lucid interval, he contract matrimony, it is not true matrimony, because consent is required in order to matrimony, and where the use of reason is wanting there cannot be consent.

This impediment is included under the head of error.

CCCCLXXI. The principal good of matrimony is the education of offspring for the worship of God. This education is a work common to both father and mother. If they be of different religions, each will intend to bring up their joint offspring in his or her own faith; and so the intentions of the two being contrary the one to the other, they may *not* fittingly be joined together in holy matrimony. Wherefore disparity of religion preceding matrimony is an impediment to its being contracted.

CCCCLXXIII. Joseph, and Moses, and Esther contracted matrimony with unbelievers, but with this difference in their case. Under the Old Law, wedlock was permitted to the Israelites with certain unbelievers, and prohibited with others. It was specially prohibited with the unbelievers dwelling in the land of Canaan, for one reason, because the Lord had commanded them to be slain for their obstinacy; for another, because of the imminent peril of unbelieving wives perverting them to idolatry, to which the children of Israel were all the more prone from their residence in the midst of idolaters. But it was permitted to the Israelites to contract matrimony with other Gentiles, especially when there was no fear of perversion to idolatry; hence the marriages of Joseph, Moses, and Esther, and the precept as to Gentile women taken captive in war.

CCCCLXXIV. If one of the faithful contract matrimony with a baptized heretick, it is true matrimony, although he sins thereby if he knew her to be a heretick, as he would sin if he should contract with an excommunicated woman. But the marriage would not therefore be dissolved. Suppose a catechumen holding the right faith, but not yet baptized, should contract with a baptized woman, it would not be true matrimony; matrimony being a sacrament, and so, in order to its reception requiring previous baptism, baptism being the gate of the sacraments (*Janua sacramentorum*).

What fellowship, asks S. Paul of the Corinthians, hath light with darkness? But the fellowship between a man and his wife is the closest and most intimate of all. And so he who dwells in the light of faith may not contract matrimony with her who has her abode in the darkness of unbelief.

CCCCLXXV. Between infidels there may exist true matrimony, and so, since no impediment *supervening* to true matrimony, destroys it, the conversion of one of the parties to the faith does not thereby loose the bond of matrimony. But sometimes, the bond of matrimony remaining, the matrimony is dissolved as to cohabitation and payment of the marriage debt when there occurs *pari passu* infidelity and adultery, both being contrary to the good of offspring. Hence as he has it in his power to put away the adulteress or to remain with her; so he has it also in his power to put away an unbelieving wife or to remain with her. For an innocent man may freely remain with an adulteress, in the hope of her reformation, although not if she be obstinate in her sin of adultery, lest he appear the patron of her shame; albeit, at the same time, he may as freely put her away, even although there be hope of her reformation. Similarly a faithful convert may dwell with an unbelieving wife in the hope of her conversion, if she appear not to be obstinate in her infidelity. And he does well in so remaining with her, albeit he is not *bound* to do so.

S. Paul counselled the Corinthians, If any brother hath a wife that believeth not, and she be pleased to dwell with him, let him not put her away. And the woman which hath an husband that believeth not, and if he be pleased to dwell with her, let her not leave him. For the unbelieving husband is sanctified by the wife; and the unbelieving wife is sanctified by the husband. But if the unbelieving depart, let him depart.

CCCCLXXVI. Unbaptized infidels are not bound by the Statutes of the Church, of which they are not members, but they are bound by the Statutes of the Divine Law, in as much as they are God's creatures; and so if, during their infidelity, they have contracted matrimony within the degrees forbidden by the Divine Law, as laid down in the Book of Leviticus, their cohabition must cease on the conversion of either or both to the Christian faith. But if they have in the time past of their infidelity contracted matrimony within the degrees forbidden only by the Statutes of the Church, they may continue to live together if both be converted, or if one be converted, and there be a reasonable hope of the conversion of the other.

CCCCLXXVII. Those things which are competent to and expedient for a man differ according to his estate in life. He, therefore, who is dead to his first life, is not held bound to those things to which he was bound in that first life. For instance, he, who while living a secular life, vowed certain things, is not bound to do them when he becomes dead to the world by entering on the religious life. Now he who comes to Baptism is born again in Christ, and dies to his former life, and so is freed from his previous obligation to his wife to pay her the marriage debt, and is not *bound* to cohabit with her when she refuses to be converted. In any case, however, he is free to do so, as has been said and shewn; even as also a religious may freely perform the vows which he made while yet in the world, so they be not contrary to the religion he has entered, although he is not *bound* to do so.

A woman has power over her husband's body only so long as he lives. When he dies to his former life, the power she had obtained during that life ceases. The husband being dead, she is, as S. Paul says, loosed from the law of her husband. By his ceasing to cohabit with her, therefore, on his conversion, and her obstinate adherence to her unbelief, she suffers no wrong. Nay, she suffers by her own fault who refuses to be turned from the error of her ways.

He who passes from the secular life to the religious dies to his former life by a spiritual only, and not by a corporal death; and so, if the matrimony have been consummated, the husband cannot, without consent of the wife, pass to religion, although he can before carnal *copula*, the only bond between them until then being a spiritual one.

But he who comes to Baptism is not spiritually only, but also *even corporally* buried with Christ unto His death; and so he is loosed from his obligation to pay the marriage debt, even after his matrimony has been consummated.

When one of the spouses is converted to the faith, the other continuing in unbelief—even if the unbelieving spouse be willing to cohabit without contumely of the Creator, and without endeavouring to reduce the other to unbelief—he or she may notwithstanding freely leave the other's society, but may not marry a third party. If, however, the unbelieving spouse will not cohabit without contumely of the Creator by words of blasphemy, without despising the name of Christ, or without endeavouring to reduce the other to unbelief, that other may not only leave the unbelieving spouse but may marry a third party in the faith of Christ.

CCCCLXXVIII. In no case may a man of his own authority slay his adulterous wife without rendering himself liable to everlasting punishment; although he may, if moved by righteous zeal, and not by hatred or revenge, without sin denounce her to the civil courts, hand her over to the secular arm, and demand the punishment of death decreed by the law for her adultery.

Neither according to the Civil Law, the Ecclesiastical Law, nor the Law of Conscience, may a man slay his adulterous wife, not taken in the act of adultery, even although he know her to be an adulteress.

The Civil Law regards as lawful the slaughter of a wife taken by her husband in the very act of adultery—not, indeed, as prescribing this course of action, but as refraining from the infliction of the punishment of homicide on such an one by reason of the greatness of his provocation.

But the Church of God, to whom has been committed not the material but the spiritual sword, is not bound by human laws so as to prevent her visiting the uxoricide with her censures, and judging him to be worthy of eternal punishment.

There are two congregations of men—the one œconomick, as the family; the other politick, as the city or kingdom. He who is set over the second congregation—the King has power to punish, not only for the correction of the individual, but for the welfare of the community committed to his care. He who is set over the first congregation, the *Paterfamilias*, has power to punish, but only so as to correct the individual members of his family. A man, therefore, may chasten his wife, but he may not slay her.

CCCCLXXIX. A man who has slain his wife may not, according to the Church's law, marry another, unless, in order to avoid fornication, he obtain a dispensation. But if, without the dispensation, he have contracted matrimony, although he sins as transgressing the commandment of the Church, yet the contract is not destroyed, unless he have married a woman with whom he has previously committed fornication.

CCCCLXXX. Since no one can make an offering to God of that which is another's and not his own; and the body of the one spouse is, after the matrimony has been consummated, in the power of the other, neither may, without consent of the other, offer his or her body to God by a vow of continence.

Again, no one may lawfully do aught which is to the prejudice of another without that other's consent, but for one spouse to enter religion might be to the prejudice of the other spouse, and is, therefore, without that other's consent, unlawful. S. Paul teaches that not even to give themselves to fasting and prayer for a time, may one *defraud* the other, except it be *with consent*.

CCCCLXXXI. Before their carnal union there exists between the spouses only a spiritual bond, but after it there is also between them a carnal bond. As after carnal union the carnal bond of matrimony is loosed by carnal death so after only spiritual union the spiritual bond of matrimony is loosed by spiritual death. The religious life is a spiritual death; he who thereby dieth to the world liveth unto God. The matrimony of the spouses is therefore dissolved by the spiritual death of either—that is, by either entering religion *before* their matrimony has been carnally consummated.

CCCCLXXXI. Matrimony, *before* carnal union, signifies that conjunction which is effected between Christ and the individual soul by grace, but which may be dissolved by a contrary spiritual disposition, that is, by mortal sin. Matrimony, *after* carnal union, signifies the conjunction effected between Christ and His Church by His assumption of human nature into the unity of His Person; and this union is altogether indivisible.

CCCCLXXXII. Before carnal union the body of the one spouse has not been wholly transferred into the power of the other; by carnal union the transference is completed: each then enters on corporal possession of the power delivered by the other. Until this completion of the transference, there is place for deliberation as to entrance on another and a higher life.

CCCCLXXXIII. As the corporal death of the man dissolves the matrimonial bond in such-wise that, according to the judgment of the Apostle, the woman may marry whom she will; so, also, after the spiritual death of the man, by his entrance into religion before consummation of matrimony, the woman may marry whom she will.

No man, in obliging himself, can oblige another to the counsels of perfection; and so no man, by entering religion, can thereby oblige his wife to continence.

CCCCLXXXIV. The Lord permitted a man to put away his wife for fornication, for the punishment of her who had broken faith, and for the relief of him who had preserved it. But there are seven cases in which it is not lawful for a man to put away his fornicating wife; in these either the wife is free from fault, or both are equally blameable—1, If the man himself has likewise committed fornication; 2, if he has himself prostituted his wife; 3, if the wife has married another, believing, with probability, her husband to be dead by reason of his long absence; 4, if she has been unwittingly known by another man personating her husband; 5, if she has been overcome by force; 6, if the husband has reconciled himself to his wife, by carnal knowledge of her, after his acquaintance with her adultery; 7, if, the matrimony having been contracted during the infidelity of both, the husband has given the wife a writ of repudiation, and she has married another, for then, on the conversion of both, he is bound to receive her back.

CCCCLXXXV. If a man put away his fornicating wife through lust of revenge, he sins; but not if he put her away—1, to avoid his own infamy, lest he appear a partaker of her crime; 2, or for her correction; 3, or to avoid uncertainty as to his offspring.

CCCCLXXXVI. Fornication is directly contrary to the goods of matrimony, for by it—1, there arises uncertainty as to offspring; 2, faith is broken; and 3, the sacramental signification fails when one of the spouses divides his body among many. It is as such that fornication is a cause of divorce, while other crimes, perchance more grievous, but not so opposed to the ends of matrimony, are not.

Unbelief, which is called spiritual fornication, is also contrary to a good of matrimony, to wit, the education of offspring for the worship of God. It also causes divorce; but otherwise than does corporal fornication. One act of carnal fornication is a cause of divorce, but not one act of spiritual fornication or unbelief—there is required a succession of acts which form a habit and imply pertinacious obstinacy.

CCCCLXXXVII. If the adulteress repent her of her adultery, her husband is not bound, of precept, to put her away; but if she be incorrigible, and persist therein, he must put her away, lest he be partaker of her sins—for he cannot be at once the head of an harlot and a member of Christ.

Divorce was permitted for the correction and amendment of the adulteress, but correcting punishment is not needed where amendment has gone before. Correction, moreover, may be made by words and blows, and where these are found sufficient, the greater punishment is not necessary.

CCCCLXXXVIII. A man may put away his wife, if *from his bed only*, of his own accord, as soon as he discovers her fornication; neither is he bound to pay her the marriage debt, even if she demand it, unless he be compelled by the Church. In that case, his payment of it will be without prejudice to himself.

But a man cannot put away his wife from both bed and *cohabitation*, without a sentence of the Church, which is called a Divorce.

The spouses are equally bound to mutual fidelity; and so the infidelity of either is an equal cause of divorce. But as regards the good of offspring, the adultery of the wife is a greater cause of divorce than the adultery of the husband, from the consequent confusion and uncertainty as to the paternity of her offspring.

CCCCLXXXIX. No subsequent adultery can cause the marriage to be other than true matrimony; and so neither of the spouses can, during the lifetime of the other, marry a third person.

No one ought to derive advantage from sin. But if the adulterer or adulteress might marry his or her paramour, it would not only be deriving advantage from their sin, but the prospect of it would be no mean incentive thereto.

CCCCXC. A man may recal and be reconciled to the wife he has put away, on her repentance. But if she be incorrigible, he may no more recal her than, as has been shewn, he may retain her, lest he become partaker of her sin.

The Church's sentence of divorce did not compel, but merely permitted, the separation of the spouses. And so their reconciliation may take place without any retractation of that sentence.

CCCCXCI. The marriage bond lasts till, but not beyond, the death of the spouses; and so, on the death of either, the other may contract a second marriage with a third person; and a third marriage with a fourth person, and so on as often as the marriage bond is loosed by death.

A second marriage is said to be—not good; not as unlawful, but as lacking the honourable significance of a first marriage, which, by its union of one man and one woman, represents the union and unity of Christ and the one Church, which is His Bride.

Wherever there are found the essentials of a sacrament, there is there a true sacrament. These are found in second marriages equally as in first. They are—1, due matter—two lawful persons, man and woman; 2, due form —the expression of their inward consent by outward words *de præsenti*.

CCCCXCII. The nuptial benediction is withheld—1, from the second marriage of a widower with a widow; 2, and from the first marriage of a man with a widow; 3, but not from the second marriage of a widower with a virgin, which has in some sort a sacramental significance, because although Christ has but one spouse, to wit, the Church, yet are there many persons espoused in that one Church. But the soul, signified by the woman, cannot be the spouse of another than Christ, signified by the man, and so the nuptial benediction is withheld from the wedding of a widow—whether with a widower or a previously unmarried man.

CCCCXCIII. Cum sacrum conjugium institutum sit ut vitetur fornicatio, et ut liberis opera detur, tenentur conjuges ad debitum sibi mutuo reddendum, quatenus utriusque incolumitas id patitur; alioquin non debiti petitio sed injusta exactio est.

Sicut servus est in potestate domini sui, ita etiam unus conjugum in potestate alterius; et ex necessitate precepti, Reddite omnibus debitum, tenetur alteri debitum reddere.

Redditione debiti medicamentum præstatur contra uxoris concupiscentiam: sed medicus cui infirmus est commissus, tenetur morbo ejus subvenire, etiam si ipse non petat. Præterea, prælatus tenetur correctionis remedium contra peccatum subditorum adhibere, etiam eis contradicentibus. Vir ergo, ut medicus, necnon ut prælatus tenetur uxori debitum reddere, etiam non petenti.

Petere debitum contingit dupliciter; uno modo *expressè*, ut quando verbis invicem petunt: alio modo, *intemperativè*, quando scilicet, vir percipit per aliqua signa quod uxor vellet sibi debitum reddi, sed propter verecundiam, cùm naturâ mulieres sint verecundae, tacet. His signis apparentibus, tenetur vir uxori etiam non expressè petenti debitum reddere. Sed contra uxor non tenetur viro debitum reddere, nisi petat.

Matrimonium, cùm sit conjunctio, est relatio æquiparantiæ; ideo, ut dicit Apostolus, vir sui corporis potestatem non habet, et similitèr dicitur de uxore; ergo, sunt æquales in actu matrimonii.

Scriptum est, Nolite fraudare invicem, nisi ex consensu ad tempus, ut vacetis orationi. Præterea, nullus potest facere votum de alieno, cùm vovere voluntatis sit, ut etiam ipsum nomen ostendit; unde de illis tantum bonis potest esse votum quae nostrae subjacent voluntati. Sed conjuges sibi invicem teneantur in redditione debiti, ita ut vir non habeat potestatem sui corporis sed uxor, et uxor non habeat potestatem sui corporis sed vir. Ergo non potest vir aut uxor absque mutuo consensû votum continentiæ facere, vel simplicitèr, vel ad tempus. Si voverit, peccat; et non debet servare votum sed agere pænitentiam de voto malè facto.

Sicut aliqua loca sunt sacra, quia deputata sunt sacris, ita aliqua tempora sunt sacra propter eandem rationem; sed in loco sacro non licet petere debitum: ergo, nec in tempore sacro. Cum actus matrimonialis, quamvis culpâ careat, tamen, quia rationem deprimit propter carnis delectationem, hominem ad spiritualia ineptum reddat, diebus sacris in quibus præcipuè spiritualibus est vacandum, non licet petere debitum.

Non peccat *mortaliter*, aut vir aut uxor si debitum diebus festis petat ; si tamen hoc faciat solâ delectationis causâ, graviùs peccat quam qui hoc facit ut sibi de lubrico carnis caveat.

Ne propter carnis lubricum aliquæ peccati detur occasio, tenentur conjuges, etiam diebus festis et quâcunque horâ, sibi mutuo debitum reddere, salvâ tamen debitâ honestate quae in talibus exigitur ; quia non oportet quod statim, in publico reddatur debitum.

CCCCXCIV. In all things natural there exist certain principles, or mainsprings, whereby they may not only effect their own proper operations, but also cause them to work together for their end—that is to say, for their final cause —for the end of their existence. Or, again, they may be actions which accomplish a certain result from the nature of their *genus*, or from the nature of their *species*. But as in things which act from a necessity of their nature, the principles of actions are their forms whereby their operations advance in order to their end, so in those which partake of cognition, the principles of action are cognition and appetite. Hence there must be in the cognitive power natural conception, and in the appetitive power natural inclination, whereby the operation belonging to the *genus*, or the *species*, is rendered competent to its end. But as man, from among the other animals, knows the reason of his end, and the proportion of operations in order to that end, so the natural conception with which he is endowed, and whereby he is directed to operate, is conveniently called the Natural Law (*lex naturalis vel jus naturale*). In the other animals it is called instinct (*æstimatio naturalis*). For the brutes are impelled by force of nature to the performance of fitting actions, rather than regulated by their own judgment. The Natural Law, therefore, is none other than a conception wherewith man is naturally endowed, whereby he is directed to the right performance of the actions proper to him—whether they belong to him from the nature of his *genus*, as to generate, to eat, and the like, or from the nature of his *species*, as, for instance, to reason. Now, everything which renders an action unsuitable or inappropriate to the end which Nature intends, is said to be *contrary to the Law of Nature*. Further, an action may be said to be inappropriate to its end, whether that end be principal or secondary, and, in either case, in two ways : 1. In that it wholly hinders the end—as too great superfluity or defect of food hinders the health of the body, the principal end of food, and hinders also one's fitness for the despatch of business, the secondary end of food. 2. In that it renders difficult, or less meet, the approach to the end, whether principal or secondary, as inordinate eating at undue times. If, therefore, the action be inappropriate to the end, as altogether and directly hindering the principal end, it is prohibited by the Law of Nature, being contrary to the first precepts of the Law of Nature, which are in things operable what the common conceptions of the mind are in things speculative. But if it be incompetent to the secondary end in any way, or even to the principal end, as making the approach thither difficult or less congruous, it is prohibited, not indeed by the first precepts of the Law of Nature, but by the second, which are divided from the first, as the conclusions in things speculative are derived from the principles or premises known *per se*.

1. Matrimony has for its principal end the procreation and education of offspring; which end indeed is competent to man, according to the nature of his *genus*, and hence is common to the other animals. 2. But a secondary end of matrimony—and one special and peculiar to man alone—is fellowship in those works which are necessary in domestic life. In order to this there must be mutual fidelity, which is thus another of the goods of matrimony. 3. But matrimony has yet another end, as contracted between believers, namely, to signify the union between Christ and His Church—and, therefore, a third good, to wit, its sacramentality. 1. The first end answers to the matrimony of man, as he is an *animal.* 2. The second, as he is a *man.* 3. The third, as he is a *believer.* 1. A plurality of wives then neither wholly destroys, nor in any way hinders, the first end of matrimony, since one man is sufficient to fertilize many wives, as well as to educate the children born of them. 2. But if it does not wholly destroy the second end, it at any rate grievously interferes with it; for there cannot easily be peace in a family where several wives are joined to one man, since one man cannot suffice to satisfy the desires of many wives, and also because the sharing by many of one office causes strife. 3. The third end of matrimony, its sacramental significance, it wholly destroys.

In some ways, therefore, a *plurality of wives* may be said to be *against the law of nature*, and in other ways, not so.

S. Augustine says that when it was the custom, to have more wives than one was not a sin. In explanation of this, it must be borne in mind that custom is not to the prejudice of the Law of Nature as to its first precepts. But as to the secondary precepts or conclusions drawn from these, custom either adds to, or diminishes, as the case may be, as Tully shows in his Rhetoric. Under this latter category comes the precept of the Law of Nature about unity of wives.

CCCCXCV. Inasmuch as human acts must vary according to the diverse conditions of persons and periods, and other circumstances, so the foresaid conclusions do not proceed from the first precepts of the Law of Nature, as having efficacy always, but only for the most part; and where their efficacy fails they may lawfully be pretermitted. But inasmuch as it is not easy to determine varieties of this sort, it is reserved to him from whose authority the law has efficacy, to license the pretermission of the law in such cases to which the efficacy of the law ought not to extend. Such license is called a dispensation. Now, the law of unity of wives was not of human, but of divine institution; it was never delivered verbally or in writing, but was imprinted on the heart, as were and are all things else belonging to the Law of Nature. In this matter, therefore, dispensation might be made by God alone, which was done *by internal inspiration* to the Holy Fathers in the first place, and from them, by means of their example, derived to others. This was done at that time, when it was necessary that the foresaid precept of nature should be pretermitted, in order that there might be a greater increase and multiplication of offspring to be educated for the worship of God. Nor was this unreasonable, for the principal end is to be kept in view rather than the secondary end. Now the good of offspring is the principal end of matrimony; and when, as at that time, the multiplication of offspring was necessary, it was fitting that the impediments which might arise to the secondary ends of matrimony (as has been shewn), and to remove which the precept prohibiting a plurality of wives was ordained, should be for a time neglected.

CCCCXCVI. The Advent of Christ ushered in the time of the fulness of the grace of Christ, whereby the worship of God is spread abroad among all nations by spiritual propagation. There is not, therefore, in our day the same cause for a dispensation, as existed in the old times before Christ's coming, when the worshippers of God, their company confined to the single nation of the Jews, were multiplied by carnal propagation.

CCCCXCVII. Since sexual intercourse is to be used, not for mere delectation, but for that end which nature chiefly intends—to wit, the procreation and education of offspring, so union with a concubine, the chief end of which is mere delectation, is contrary to the Law of Nature. Desire of offspring may have place in concubinage, but not their education, which implies a lengthened cohabitation and mutual care of the parents. Even those birds which nourish their offspring, do not separate till that mutual duty of nature is accomplished.

Things derive their names from their chief ends. As matrimony takes its name, as has been shewn, from its chief end, so is the name of concubine derived from the chief end for which she is sought—*concubitus*.

Those acts are mortal sins whereby is violated the bond of friendship between man and God, and man and man. As destroying the due ordination, intended by nature, of parent and offspring, simple fornication—that is, intercourse with a concubine—would, even were there no written law, be a mortal sin.

In virtue of that dispensation whereby the Old Fathers had a plurality of wives, they went in also unto their handmaids. These became their wives as to the principal and primary end of matrimony, but not as to its secondary end of domestic fellowship, with which their estate of bondage interfered, for they could not be at once companions and handmaids.

CCCCXCVIII. He who ministers the sacraments to others, that is to say, an ordained person, ought himself to be in no way sacramentally defective. But there is a defect in the sacrament when the full and entire signification of the sacrament is not found therein. Now the sacrament of matrimony signifies the union of Christ with His Church, which is a union of One with one. And so it is required, in order to the perfect signification of this sacrament, that a man be the husband of but one wife, and a woman the wife of but one husband. Bigamy, therefore, which destroys this signification, induces *irregularity*. There are four modes of bigamy—1, when a man has several wives, *de jure*, successively ; 2, when he has several wives at once, one *de jure*, another *de facto* ; 3, when he has several successively, one *de jure*, another *de facto* ; 4, when he takes a widow to wife. In all these cases there is *irregularity*.

There is another cause assigned for the impediment to orders of *irregularity*, namely, that in ordained persons there ought to be apparent the greatest spirituality, as well because they minister spiritual things as because they teach spiritual things, and ought to be occupied in spiritual things. To this spirituality, concupiscence, whereby the whole man becomes fleshly, is above all things repugnant, and its existence becomes very apparent, in those who will not be content with one wife. But the first is the better reason.

The first mode of bigamy is the *principal* cause of irregularity. The second and third modes are *secondary* causes, and are causes inasmuch as, although in the *de facto* union there is no sacrament, there is yet a similitude of sacrament.

A man marrying a woman not a virgin, even if he be ignorant of that fact, incurs irregularity, since it is not a punishment inflicted, but a sacramental defect. A man not a virgin, marrying a woman who is a virgin, does not incur irregularity.

Baptism looses from guilt and not from wedlock; but as from wedlock irregularity arises, so by baptism it is not destroyed. A baptised person is conformed to Christ as to the virtue of his mind, not as to the estate of his flesh.

The irregularity attaching to bigamy is not of the natural law, but of positive law, neither is it of the essentials of Order that the person ordained be not a bigamist, as is apparent from this—that if a bigamist be ordained he receives *character*. And so the Pope can dispense, in case of such irregularity *wholly;* but a Bishop only as to the minor orders, save in certain cases.

CCCCXCIX. Matrimony, of the intention of nature, is ordained for the education of offspring, not only for a time, but during the whole life of the offspring. Hence it is of the law of nature that parents lay up treasure for their children, and that children be the heirs of their parents. Since offspring is a good common to both husband and wife, their society must needs remain perpetually undivided, according to the dictate of the law of nature. The inseparability of matrimony is therefore of the law of nature: but is contained under the second rather than under the first precepts of that law, and so may fall under dispensation.

To repudiate a wife was not allowed, under the law of Moses, by the *commandment* of God; but by reason of the hardness of their hearts it was *permitted* to the Jews, in order to avoid greater evils, especially that of uxoricide, to which they were prone.

Since a woman, as long as she lives, is bound by the law of her husband, she cannot, even if repudiated, marry another, unless it be permitted to her by Divine dispensation.

That a man may not rashly repudiate his wife, he was forbidden to take again to wife her whom he had once put away.

The cause of the permission to repudiate a wife was the avoidance of uxoricide. But the proximate cause of homicide is hatred. And so the proximate cause of repudiation is hatred; its remote causes being the motives of hatred. The causes of repudiation were inscribed in the writ of repudiation not in special, but in general, in order that after a delay, and by the counsel of the Scribes, the man might desist from his purpose of repudiating his wife.

CCCCC. The estate of children is fourfold—1, some are natural and legitimate, as those who are born of true and lawful matrimony; 2, some are natural and not legitimate, as those who are born of simple fornication; 3, Some are legitimate but not natural, as those who have been adopted; 4, while others are neither legitimate nor natural, as those who are born of adultery, or *stuprum* (commerce with a virgin or widow, as distinguished from *adulterium*, commerce with a married woman; *fornicatio simplex*, commerce with a concubine or whore; *incestus*, commerce within the forbidden degrees; and *raptus*, forcible violation or rape). These are said to be neither legitimate nor natural, as born both contrary to positive law and expressly contrary to the law of nature.

Illegitimate offspring suffer a double loss. 1. They are not admitted to the performance of legitimate acts—that is, to the enjoyment of offices and dignities which require honourable birth in those who exercise them. 2. They do not succeed to their paternal heritage. Their parents are however bound, of natural law, to provide them a necessary maintenance, and the Bishop ought to be solicitous to compel them to do so.

What the Law does, the Law may undo. Children are declared illegitimate by positive law; and so by the same law they may be legitimized: as, for instance, by the subsequent marriage of their parents, if their previous union was not adulterous.

Laus Deo.

APPENDIX.

The Axioms of Augustinus Hunnæus,

CONCERNING

THE SACRAMENTS OF THE CHURCH OF CHRIST;

WHEREIN the doctrine of S. Thomas Aquinas concerning the same Sacraments, delivered in the iiid. part of his Theological Summa, and its Supplement, is recalled from the prolixity of disputation to that utmost brevity, which is most agreeable to the memory; with the addition of Schemes which place briefly and clearly before the eye the method which S. Thomas there follows, in explaining the matter of the Sacraments.

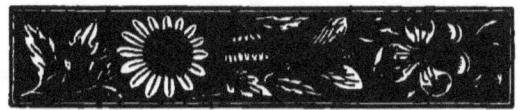

Typographus Candido Lectori. S.

ITS manifold usefulness has prevented me from omitting this little book of Aug. Hunnæus, late Regius Professor of Theology at Louvain.

1. This little book embraces one part of Theological teaching—one, too, most necessary to be known—that, namely, which pertains to the doctrine of the Sacraments, so briefly and lucidly, and if you want only a bare knowledge of the truth, withal so fully and perfectly, and in so excellent an order, that I do think there is extant neither any compendium, nor any other sort of writing, whence the student of Christian piety may more easily and more fruitfully, and with equal brevity, acquire a knowledge of that part of Theology.

2. Moreover, this little book supplies commonplaces concerning the Sacraments, digested in a most convenient order, to which you can add a reference of whatever you may note in other ecclesiastical writers, as worthy to be known and remembered concerning the same matters, and this with the utmost usefulness in the promotion of your studies.

3. To us it appears to be no small, and certainly no blameable convenience of this little book, that those things which the student of Christian piety has read in S. Thomas, or any orthodox writer, treating copiously of the Sacraments, he may here briefly and compendiously recal, and both renew and confirm his recollection of the same. *Vale et experire.*

AXIOMS OF AUGUSTINUS HUNNÆUS,

Concerning the Sacraments, briefly and lucidly embracing the whole doctrine of the iiid. part of the Summa of S. Thomas Aquinas, concerning the Seven Sacraments of the Church, distributed into ninety-nine Commonplaces.

AXIOM I.

Of the nature and proper idea of Sacraments in general.

A Sacrament is a sign, set before the senses, of a certain sacred reality, which conveys holiness to a man; which also renews the memory of Christ, and which fortells the glory of the blessedness to come. As in the several Sacraments there are to be employed, in place of matter, certain things having definite significations, so also to hold the place of form should be added to these certain definite words. Nor to these may aught be added, or from them aught subtracted, whereby the sense of a lawful form is overthrown.

AXIOM II.

The necessity of Sacraments.

During the state of innocence indeed, man needed no Sacraments, for either the healing or the perfecting of his nature. But after the loss of that desirable estate, by the fall of the first parent, Sacraments began to be necessary to men, to those who preceded the advent of Christ, in order to the profession of their faith in the Christ who should be born, and suffer; to those who thereafter were, or will be, in order to the testimony of their faith in the Christ who was born, and has suffered, and to both, in order to the attainment of the eternal salvation of their souls.

AXIOM III.

The principal effect of the Sacraments, which is Grace.

The Sacraments of the New Law, not indeed as principal causes, but as instruments of the Divine Mercy, do, by a power of their own, derived from the Passion of Christ, confer grace in such sort, that thereby there arrives, over and beyond gifts and virtues, a certain Divine aid, in order to the more easy attainment of the end of the Sacrament: whence it is clear that grace is contained in a Sacrament, as is a reality in its sign, and an effect in its instrument. The Sacraments of the Old Law were indeed certain symbols of saving faith in Christ, but in no way had they any power or efficacy to confer grace.

AXIOM IV.

The secondary effect of certain Sacraments, which is Character.

By three of the Sacraments of the New Law—Baptism, Confirmation, and Order—a certain spiritual *character* is impressed on the souls of the receivers, which is none other than a certain spiritual faculty, proceeding from God, and, in order to the right performance of the Divine worship, impressed on the intelligent part of the soul as its subject: and this can never be effaced or obliterated.

AXIOM V.

The cause of the Sacraments, or their Author and Minister.

As the Author and Institutor of the Sacraments is God alone, so likewise is He the primary and principal cause of their internal effect. Man is only their minister; and so Christ, as God, by His own authority, operates the internal effect of a Sacrament; as man, He operates by His merits, and has the power of ministry; albeit, the principal, and by far the most excellent. Hence, although the power which, as man, Christ obtained in the Sacraments, He could communicate to another man; yet the authority which, as God, He had in the same, He could impart to no mortal any more than He could His own Divinity. As to the Ministers of the Sacraments, the Catholic Church of Christ holds and teaches that the wicked sin indeed by ministering the Sacraments; but the Sacraments themselves are, by the perversity of their ministers, neither polluted nor impeded. Although the dispensation of the Sacraments might have been conceded by God to angels, it was not so conceded, but to men only. In the ministers of the Sacraments, not faith, but a right intention is necessary; and not any intention, but that only which directly respects the Sacrament itself.

AXIOM VI.

The number of the Sacraments.

There are Seven Sacraments of the Church, which have this order among themselves—Baptism holding the first place; Confirmation follows it; the Eucharist—Confirmation; Penance—the Eucharist; Extreme Unction—Penance; Order—Extreme

Unction; and Matrimony—Order. Of which Sacraments, although they are all indeed of exceeding moment, in order to the promotion of man's salvation, three only are of necessity thereto. Baptism indubitably for all men, Order for the Church, and Penance for those who after baptism have polluted themselves by any wickedness. But although, by a certain natural order, the third place among the Sacraments has been given to the Eucharist, yet in dignity and majesty it far excels all the rest.

Concerning Baptism.

Axiom VII.

Of the nature and proper idea of Baptism.

Baptism is properly a washing with water, with the addition of prescribed words. It is of the number of those Sacraments which do not admit of iteration. So far as pertains to its power, and name of Sacrament, it was instituted at the Baptism of Christ; as to the necessity of its use after His death and resurrection. Its matter is water, even although it have suffered change or mixture, so that it retain the name and appearance of water: its form: I baptise thee, in the name of the Father, and of the Son, and of the Holy Ghost. Wherefore it would not be a baptism which, without a special dispensation of God, should be conferred in the name of Christ. With regard to immersion, it is to be held that, although neither trine nor single immersion be necessary to a baptism; nay, that although effusion or aspersion with water suffice to the validity of a baptism, still, unless for the avoidance of scandal or of the customs of heretics, trine immersion may not, without grave sin, be omitted; for that is the fitting rite which, with others, the Church hath been wont to use in this Sacrament. With regard to the three kinds of baptism—which are the baptisms of water, of blood, and of the Spirit—the Church so holds that she attributes to the first the effect of baptism along with the name of the Sacrament, to the other two the effect only, and to the baptism of blood the most excellent and perfect effect.

Axiom VIII.

The Minister of Baptism.

Although the proper and ordinary minister of Baptism is not a deacon but a priest, yet in the absence of a priest, the power of baptising is, in case of urgent necessity, conceded, not only to a deacon or any cleric whomsoever, but even to a laic, a woman, and what is more, to a person not baptised. Nevertheless, every one of these would sin if, either without necessity, or in the presence of some one more nearly approaching the sacerdotal dignity, they should rashly usurp the function of baptism. Two persons, moreover, at one and the same time, so they both observe the accustomed form of the Church, may baptise one and the same person. But if, accommodating the form to themselves, they say, instead of, I baptise thee, We baptise thee, their attempt would most likely be invalid and vain. With regard to sponsors, it is to be held that he who is baptised ought to have a sponsor, as it were a pedagogue, not as a necessity of the Sacrament, but in order to a greater care of the salvation of the person to be baptised; for it pertains to the office of a sponsor, if the parents of the baptised fulfil not their duty, to endeavour that he be imbued with the sound Catholic faith, and holy and Christian morals.

AXIOM IX.

The Recipient of Baptism.

Baptism, either in deed, or in will, is universally necessary to the salvation of all men; in the case of infants it is never, in the case of adults, it is nearly always to be deferred. It has from the passion and death of Christ so great power to eradicate the stains of sin which it finds, that to no person when baptized is aught to be prescribed in name of satisfaction. But those sinners only who repent them of their faults, and not those whom the insane lust of sinning still holds captive, are to be received to this Sacrament; although there is not here required an outward confession of sins, yet there is required in order to the reception of the fruit of this Sacrament—the inward confession which is made to God, and a detestation of the previous evil life. Intention of receiving baptism is in the case of adults necessary to the reception even of *character*. Nevertheless, without right faith one may receive the *character*, but not the grace or fruit of baptism. Although, as aforesaid, this Sacrament is to be imparted to infants without delay, still the children of Jews or other infidels, not yet arrived at the use of reason, are not to be baptized against the will of their parents. Neither are idiots or mad persons, unless they have always, from their birth, laboured under these imperfections; or, before their loss of reason, signified their desire of baptism. Those who are still in their mother's womb, since they cannot be washed, clearly cannot in any way be baptized.

AXIOM X.

The Effect of Baptism.

Baptism washes away the stains of all sins which it finds, taking away the guilt at the same time with the penalty—adorns with grace and virtues, infants no less than adults, illuminates the mind, engrafts a man into the Body of Christ, and, as it were, renders him fruitful to the bringing forth of holy actions; opens likewise the gate of the heavenly kingdom; yet, for many reasons, takes not away the annoyances, torments, and griefs of the present life. Although all persons, with the same dispositions, have an equal share of the peculiar and ordinary effect of baptism, yet, in the participation of those effects of baptism, which, over and above the causes of its institution, the Divine bounty vouchsafes, there is great variety, even when the merits of the baptised are equal. This is also certain, that as, in order to the reception of the salutary effects of baptism, sincerity and integrity of mind are necessary, so by guile and perversity the same effects are hindered and prevented. Nevertheless, these impediments being afterwards removed, the baptism previously received results in its own natural effects of grace and virtues, just as if there had been no impediment.

AXIOM XI.

Circumcision.

Circumcision was a figure, and to a certain extent a preparation for the baptism that was to be. Since it embraced a profession of the faith of Christ, it was fitly instituted in Abraham, who was the first to receive the promise of the Christ who should be born, with the addition of those most meet rites which were dictated and prescribed by Him of Whose Wisdom there is no end. But the remission of original sin, and other graces, which fell to the Jews in circumcision, ought to be referred not to its own proper power, but to faith in the passion and death of Christ who was to come.

AXIOM XII.

Catechism and Exorcism.

Catechism, whereby the doctrine of the faith is delivered, ought to precede baptism; but exorcism, whereby evil spirits are expelled, and the senses opened to the perception of the mysteries of salvation, ought to precede catechism. Both—as well catechism as exorcism—pertain to the office of a priest; but he uses, in catechising, the ministry of a reader—in exorcism that of an exorcist.

OF THE SACRAMENT OF CONFIRMATION.

AXIOM XIII.

Confirmation is rightly numbered among the Seven Sacraments—since, as does baptism, it imprints character; and, since, as do all the other Sacraments, it imparts grace. It is, therefore, to be denied to no fit person; and it is not to be ministered by any but a Bishop. The fitting matter of this (Sacrament) is chrism—consecrated by a Bishop—the form, I sign thee with the sign of the cross, and I confirm thee with the chrism of salvation—in the Name of the Father, and of the Son, and of the Holy Ghost. The place where it ought to be applied is the forehead, as the seat of fear and shame. These rites and all others observed in this Sacrament, are most meet. Although no one, unless baptized, is fit for the receiving of confirmation, yet in confirmation, as in baptism, there ought to be present those who will undertake the office of instructing the confirmed—not indeed in the first rudiments of the Christian faith—but in those arts which are necessary to victory in the Christian and spiritual warfare.

OF THE EUCHARIST.

AXIOM XIV.

The Sacrament of the Eucharist.

Although the Eucharist, by reason of the various significations which it contains within itself, is rightly called by many names,—and by reason of the many things which it embraces, was foreshadowed by various figures, whereof the chief was the immolation of the Paschal Lamb,—it is yet one single Sacrament. It was, for many and most grave reasons, instituted by Christ at the Last Supper. It is necessary to man's salvation— not indeed *simpliciter* (by actual reception), but *exparte rei*, (as incorporating into the unity of the mystical body).

AXIOM XV.

The Matter of the Eucharist.

The legitimate matter of the Sacrament of the Eucharist is bread—wheaten—it may be either leavened or unleavened; and wine expressed from grapes, to which, when it is offered, ought to be added, a little water—not of necessity to the Sacrament—but to signify the union with Christ of His faithful people. And the quantity of these is to be fixed and determined by the use and number of those faithful who are to receive the Sacrament.

AXIOM XVI.

Transubstantiation.

In the Sacrament of the Eucharist, the bread is so converted into the True Body of Christ, and the wine into His True Blood, in a moment of time, that after the consecration, their accidents alone remaining, there is left nothing of their substance. Whence it is clear that the proposition, From bread is made the Body of Christ, albeit restrained by the properties of language, is agreeable to the truth.

AXIOM XVII.

The mode whereby Christ is in the Eucharist.

In the Sacrament of the Eucharist, not only under either.species of Bread and Wine, but also under any part of either species, be the Host broken or entire, there exists Whole Christ, with all the dimensions of His Body. Yet the Body of Christ is not contained in this Sacrament as a dimensive quantity and in a place, but as a substance under a dimensive quantity. Neither is It transferred from place to place with the removal of the Host, *per se*, but *per accidens* only. By no sense of the body—not even by the imagination, may It, as It is in this Sacrament, be perceived, but by the mind only. But when there is in this Sacrament, seen by miracle, after the consecration, either flesh or a body, since this takes place by a change in colour and figure, or in the imagination of the beholder, the dimensions of the Host remaining, it is to be believed that there is, under the accidents, the verity of the Body of Christ.

AXIOM XVIII.

The Accidents of Bread and Wine in the Eucharist.

In the Sacrament of the Eucharist, after the stupendous conversion of the substance of the bread and wine into the Lord's Body, there remains, by miracle, a dimensive quantity, to which the other accidents adhere, not only unimpaired, without a subject, but preserving also the properties and functions of matter; wherefore something may therefrom be generated and nourished. That the external body is changed, that it may be broken and corrupted with the other accidents, occurs, of its own nature, short of a miracle. The Body of Christ remains under these accidents when changed, so long as the substance of bread and wine would have remained the same in number. And so, if into the consecrated wine aught of another liquid be poured, so there be not made an universal mixture, under the part mixed there will indeed cease to be, but under the other part free from mixture, there will remain the true Blood of Christ.

AXIOM XIX.

The Form of the Eucharist.

The lawful and fitting form of the Sacrament of the Eucharist is—in the consecration of the bread—This is My Body ; in the transmutation of the wine, the words which follow—This is the chalice of My Blood of the New and Everlasting Testament, the mystery of faith, which is shed for you and for many, for the remission of sins. And the words of these forms are not only most true, but they are also the instruments of the Divine power, by a creative force infused into them, in effecting the wonderful conversion of the bread and wine into the Lord's Body. It is clear that the effect of the consecration of the bread is prior in time to the effect of the consecration of the wine.

AXIOM XX.

The Effects of the Eucharist.

The Sacrament of the Eucharist both imparts grace for the present, and for the future is of great avail to the attainment of eternal glory. For although It does not take away deadly sins, which still hold bound the man who knows of and wills the same ; yet the venial sins which It finds, and those deadly sins also which have passed from the memory, It destroys and washes away from the soul. As to the penalty remaining after the guilt is remitted, It frees therefrom only in proportion as there is an affection of charity on the part either of the offerer or the receiver of this Sacrament. It fortifies a man worthily receiving the same, as a certain salutary medicine against the always impending peril of sins. Nor does It profit only those who receive, but those also for whom It is offered. Neither past venial sins hinder Its force, nor even present, except in this way, that a soul pure from all stain of sin, this Sacrament is wont to bathe in the joy of spiritual sweetness.

AXIOM XXI.

The Reception of the Eucharist.

The idea of receiving the Sacrament of the Eucharist is twofold; one sacramental, the other spiritual. That mode which is called spiritual is peculiar to a just man; and, to an adult, is necessary for salvation. Concerning the sacramental idea of receiving, this is to be held, that not the just only, but sinners also, share in this reception, and they therein commit a grave, albeit not the gravest of all sins. To a public sinner, even though he demand it, but not to one whose sin is hidden, the Eucharist is to be denied by the priest. He who receives the Eucharist, having undergone a nocturnal pollution, sins gravely if it be the result of a previous mortal sin, but venially, if it arise from another cause, and be neither of constant nor daily occurrence. The Eucharist to be taken before all meat and drink, unless by reason of sore disease, peril of death be apprehended. In the case of mental disease, to those only is the Eucharist to be given whose life is in danger, and who have previously given some sign of a wish to receive this Sacrament. After due and sufficient preparation of the soul, this Sacrament may be rightly received, and this may be done either daily or at longer intervals. The practice of those churches is to be commended which prescribe the reception of this Sacrament by the priests under both species, but impart It to the other people, from the risk of spilling, under the species of bread only.

AXIOM XXII.

The Mode in which Christ used the Eucharist.

Christ himself received His own Body—It being yet liable to wounds and death—and also gave It to be received by His disciples, along with Judas. Since what pertains to Christ so pertains without respect to externals, it is rightly believed that the same pertains to Him existing under the veil of this Sacrament. The consequence is—that, if any one had in any place reserved the Eucharist during the time of Christ's death, Christ would have died therein no less than on the Cross.

AXIOM XXIII.

The Minister of the Eucharist.

The consecration of the Sacrament of the Eucharist is peculiar to a Priest, and cannot be effected by any other. More priests than one, whose intention refers to one moment of time, may consecrate one and the same host. Every priest ought sometimes to perform this divine function. He ought himself, after the consecration, to receive the Eucharist. Not only a virtuous priest, but also an evil priest—a schismatic—one under anathema—a heretic—nay, even a degraded priest—has power to consecrate the Body and Blood of the Lord ; but the last four may neither themselves use that power, nor may others be present, during their use thereof, without sin. Evil priests do indeed themselves sin in performing this Divine office ; but others, in hearing the same, or in receiving from them the Sacraments, incur no guilt, so that the exercise of their power have not been taken from these priests, by authority of the Church. The masses of good priests are to be preferred—not, indeed, by reason of the consecration, but for the merits of their prayers—to the masses of other priests. The distribution of this Sacrament so pertains to the office of a priest, that the distribution of the Blood is conceded to a deacon, by reason of the propinquity which he has to the sacerdotal dignity.

AXIOM XXIV.

The Rites of the Eucharist.

From the third hour to the ninth—between which Christ suffered His heaviest torments—has been reckoned the fitting time for the celebration of the Sacrament of the Eucharist, which, as well by reason of its being a representation as by reason of its effects, is rightly called an immolation of Christ. Nor is that constitution less laudable whereby, on account of the reverence due to so great a Sacrament, it has been ordained that the solemnity of the sacrifice be performed in a consecrated place, when no necessity urges otherwise ; or, there being urgent necessity, at least upon a consecrated altar, with the Bishop's consent—the consecrated vessels being always used. Wherefore, both these and all things else which, in the celebration of masses, are either said or done, were instituted for great and wise considerations ; and although divers and various accidents may happen, yet they may all be met by the prudence of the holy and sagacious overseers of the Church.

OF THE SACRAMENT OF PENANCE.

AXIOM XXV.

Penance as a Sacrament.

Penance, wherein, according to the rite of the Catholick Church, a priest, as the minister of God, absolves those who confess their sins, is a true Sacrament, rightly and meetly instituted under the new law. The proximate matter thereof is the act of the penitent—the remote, the sins themselves—its form, I absolve thee in the name of the Father, and of the Son, and of the Holy Ghost. In the pronouncing thereof, the imposition of the hand is rightly—still, not of necessity—employed. This Sacrament is not of necessity for salvation to a man *simpliciter*, but to him who has sinned—at least, in so far as it comprehends sorrow of soul for sin committed, which sorrow the sinner ought to continue—at least, by way of habit—so long as he lives. This Sacrament is, therefore, rightly called by the sacred doctors—the second plank after the shipwreck: to which plank, moreover, not once only, but as many times as it is cast adrift by the billows of fresh sins, the Christian soul may flee for refuge.

AXIOM XXVI.

Penance as a Virtue.

Penance, forasmuch as it contains a praiseworthy moderation of grief for sin committed inasmuch as it is an offence to God, together with a purpose of amendment of life, is a virtue—and a special virtue—lying under Justice as its genus, coming after Faith and Hope in order both of Nature and Time, but following Charity in the order of Nature only, not of Time. Its originating cause is fear, and that as well servile fear as ingenuous. Its subject is the will of the penitent.

AXIOM XXVII.

The effects of Penance in the destruction of Mortal Sins.

Penance, inasmuch as it is a virtue, and still more inasmuch as it is a Sacrament, remits sin. But as there is no crime of man so great that, in the present life, it cannot be destroyed by penance; so in like manner without penance, at least in so far as it is a virtue, can no deadly sin committed by man, after the use of reason, be remitted. One sin cannot be destroyed by penance, without the rest, supposing that others exist in the same man. Although by the sacrament of penance be remitted the deadly guilt, along with the eternal punishment due thereto, there yet remains the obligation to pay the temporal penalty, and certain evil dispositions contracted in consequence of the past sin.

AXIOM XXVIII.

The effects of Penance in the destruction of Venial Sins.

In order to the remission of venial sin, penance is in some sort necessary, but not an infusion of new grace. And so venial sins are remitted by a simple sprinkling with holy water, proceeding from grace, and accompanied by an expressed or at least tacit detestation of the said sins. If, however, there exist in any man venial sins conjointly with mortal, there can not be remission of the former without the latter.

AXIOM XXIX.

The return of Sins once remitted.

A deadly sin once destroyed by Penance returns with subsequent deadly sin, not indeed altogether, but inasmuch as it contained a privation of divine grace, and an obligation of undergoing eternal punishment. But, although this may be truly said of the harm following every capital sin, yet, in a certain special manner is it true of fraternal hatred, apostacy, contempt of confession, and sorrow for past performance of penance. But this is not to be taken as if, for a subsequent offence, the sinner were to be bound by guilt and penalty equal to, and the same as those by which he was previously bound, but, according as the guilt and penalty of the subsequent offence correspond to its genus, and, according to the magnitude of the ingratitude therewith conjoined. Neither is it to be supposed that the ingratitude attaching to a subsequent offence is always a special sin; but then only when the subsequent offence infers contempt of God and the benefits received from Him: in other words, that ingratitude is not the perpetration of another special sin, but an aggravation of the former offence.

AXIOM XXX.

The power of Penance towards the recovery of Lost Virtues.

Virtues lost, and in a manner extinct by reason of sin, are restored by the Sacrament of penance—sometimes in equal, sometimes in less, sometimes even in greater measure, according to the dispositions of the penitent; and the works of these so revive as to be held in the same estimation in the sight of God as before. And so, although a state of innocence once lost may not be repaired, and although certain ecclesiastical dignities are by certain crimes lost beyond hope of recovery, yet a man, by means of the Sacrament of Penance, may recover his former dignity in the sight of God. Nevertheless, the force and operation of this Sacrament is not to be extended so as to render dead actions, (praiseworthy indeed generically, but not flowing from the fountains of charity, and the state of grace), living, and efficaciously meritorious of eternal life.

AXIOM XXXI.

The Parts of Penance in genere.

Penance, as a Sacrament, consists of three parts—sorrow of soul or contrition, confession, and satisfaction. As it is a virtue, it has under it these two species—Penance before Baptism, and Penance after Baptism—which is further distributed, intopenance for deadly and penance for venial sins.

That which follows is taken from the Supplement to the IIIrd part of the Summa, which S. Thomas, overtaken by death, left imperfect.

AXIOM XXXII.

The Nature and proper idea of Contrition.

Contrition is a sorrow of soul for sin previously committed, together with a purpose of confession and satisfaction; and, seeing this springs from virtue, and from a will which detests the sin, it is clear that their opinion is false and absurd who supposed that attrition could afterwards become contrition.

AXIOM XXXIII.

The Object of Contrition.

Contrition has respect neither to the evil of the penalty of sin, nor to original sin, nor to another's sin, nor to future sin, but only to one's own sin, and that past sin. So that the sinner ought to suffer Contrition for the guilt of those sins committed in the past, as well venial as mortal, which, by the use of due diligence, occur to his memory, and of all others as they return thereto.

AXIOM XXXIV.

How great ought Contrition to be.

Contrition, as it exists in the higher appetite, produces a sorrow greater than all other sorrows, but as it exists in the lower, and also, by reason of the diversity of sins, it ought to be now greater, now less. Although in the higher appetite, or will, it can never be too great; yet, as it is in the lower, there may be excess, and therefore ought to be moderation, in order that due regard be had at once to life, and that measure of health, &c., necessary for the due performance of one's duty.

AXIOM XXXV.

The Period of Contrition.

Although contrition ought to endure throughout the whole period of the present life, and should, so far as the practice of other virtues permits, be continuous, yet to souls separated from their bodies, whatever place or state they may arrive at, there is left no room for contrition.

AXIOM XXXVI.

The Effect of Contrition.

Contrition, both as *part* of a Sacrament, and as proceeding from virtue, is the cause of the remission of sin. Nay, so great force has it, that, although small, it has power to destroy great and virulent sin, and to take away at once the guilt and the penalty attaching thereto.

AXIOM XXXVII.

The Necessity of Confession.

To the sinner bound by deadly sin, Confession, made outwardly or, where that may not be possible, made inwardly, with the desire of the other, is of necessity to salvation. Not the supreme Pontiff himself can release any one from this obligation, which is *jure Divino*. Those who have committed some grievous sin may defer its external confession till the time appointed by the Church, except on the approach of death, or in peril thereof, or unless something occur, preparatory to which Confession is necessary to be made. Those who are guilty of only slight offences ought, however, to confess these, not indeed of necessity sacramentally, but by reason of the Church's precept; or they ought, at least, to indicate the state of their conscience to their own priest. In either case, they must diligently guard against confessing or accusing themselves of any feigned offence.

AXIOM XXXVIII.
Definition of Confession.

Confession is an act of virtue, and of that virtue above-called Penance. It is not inaptly thus defined by Augustine : Confession is that wherein, by the hope of pardon, the hidden disease is laid bare.

AXIOM XXXIX.
The Minister of Confession.

Although lawful and Sacramental Confession must of necessity be made to a priest—and, with a few special exceptions, not to any priest, but to one's own—yet, in urgent necessity, he who confesses to a laic all his sins—and, necessity not urging, he who confesses to a laic lighter faults—respectively obtains pardon from God. The excepted cases, are privilege or command of a superior, or instant peril of death—under pressure of which, not only from his sins, but from the bond of any excommunication, the penitent may be absolved by any priest whomsoever. Concerning the penalty to be prescribed in place of satisfaction, since regard is to be had therein, not only to what is due, but also to remedy, the greatest penalty is not always inflicted for the greatest guilt.

AXIOM XL.
The Quality of Confession.

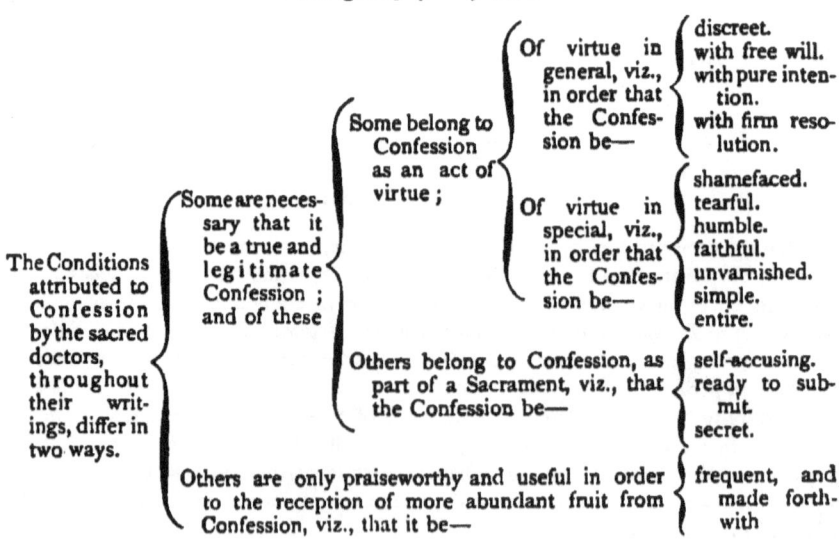

Although it is laid down among these conditions, that Confession ought to be tearful, and have united therewith sorrow for a past evil life, yet a feigned confession, that is to say, one made without the will to sin being laid aside, is not always to be iterated, but the sin of fiction is always to be afterwards confessed. When it is said that a confession must be entire, it is to be understood that the penitent confess all the sins of which he is conscious, to one priest, in expressed words, not by nod, or by writing, or through an interpreter, unless he be deaf.

AXIOM XLI.

The Effects of Confession.

Special sacramental Confession frees the penitent, not only from guilt, and, in some measure, from penalty, but it also opens to him the entrance to the heavenly kingdom, and imparts the hope of eternal salvation. General sacramental Confession has power great enough to destroy mortal sins, which, without the penitent's fault, have passed to oblivion.

AXIOM XLII.

The Seal of Confession.

A priest who reveals to others what has been said to him under the seal of confession, sins most grievously, and is a violator of a sacrament. Although this seal is peculiar to a priest, yet as Confession itself is in certain cases communicated to a laic, so is also its seal. It has respect properly and directly indeed to sins only, and those heard in sacramental confession. Still, all things which by Confession are known are diligently to be hidden both by priest and laic. Nevertheless, both priest and laic may tell to others what they have heard in Confession, if power of so doing have been granted them by the penitent; and without this power, when they ascertain in another way what has been said to them in Confession.

AXIOM XLIII.

Definition of Satisfaction.

Satisfaction is properly a compensation made for an injury inflicted, according as the equity of justice demands. Rightly, likewise, says Augustine: Satisfaction is the excision of the causes of sins, and the non-indulgence of approach to their suggestions. From both of these definitions, it is clear that Satisfaction is an act of virtue and of justice.

AXIOM XLIV.

Man can satisfy God.

Although nothing so great can be rendered by man as is the violation of the Divine Majesty, nevertheless, mortal men, when they offer what is in them, can satisfy both for their own, and, so far as pertains to the payment of debt, even for the sins of others.

AXIOM XLV.

The Quality of Satisfaction.

No man retaining one mortal sin can expiate another by Satisfaction, for the works which otherwise would have power of satisfying, if they be done—while any sin has possession of the soul—do neither then, nor afterwards, on the recovery of charity, avail aught towards satisfying. It is not, however, to be supposed that works of this sort are wholly useless, for they conduce to the acquirement of the goods of this present life, the avoidance of evils, and the formation of habits of honest dealing. They likewise dispose the soul towards the reception of grace ; and, seeing they hinder many sins, they are rightly said in some manner to mitigate and diminish the pains of Hell.

AXIOM XLVI.

Satisfactory Works.

A laudable work of satisfaction ought to have regard to the honour of God, and be of the number of those things which inflict pain. Of such sort are alms, fasting, and prayer. Afflictions also, and adversities whatsoever, sent of God, so they are borne with a steadfast and patient mind, have power of satisfying.

AXIOM XLVII.

Who are capable of Penance ?

The innocent, endowed with that grace whereby they follow all virtue while they are yet in this mortal life, have only the habit of Penance ; but the Blessed, inhabiting the heavenly country, may have also its acts. The angels, be they good or bad, are capable of neither habits nor acts of this virtue.

AXIOM XLVIII.

Definition and Division of the Keys.

There is in the Church a Key, which is rightly defined by the doctors as a power of binding and loosing, whereby the ecclesiastical judge admits the worthy, and excludes the unworthy, from the Kingdom. And this Key is twofold: one to discern, another to judge. Both of these exist in God, by authority; in Christ, by merit and excellency; in the priests of the Church—the dispensers of the Sacraments—by ministry.

AXIOM XLIX.

The Effects of the Keys.

As the baptismal water is an inanimate instrument, so is the priest, by the power of the keys committed to him, an animate instrument, which God uses in order to free man from his sins. The power of the keys given to priests extends not only to the remission of guilt, but to the diminution of that temporal penalty whereunto the eternal penalty has been commuted; and to the prescription of some other penalty, as a remedy for sin; and herein chiefly appears the power of binding. This power is to be regulated by the greatest prudence, and, according to the will and ordination of God—for otherwise it would both fail of its effect on the penitent, and redound in grievous evil on the head of the priest who abused it.

AXIOM L.

The Ministers of the Keys.

According to a twofold distinction of the keys, that which is called the key of order, exists in the priests of the New Law solely; and in all, even wicked priests: and in Christ, so much the more excellently than in any other priest, as the power of him who acts *per se* is more perfect and noble than that of an assistant instrument. Schismatics, heretics, persons excommunicated or degraded, are deprived of the use of this key, inasmuch as their subjects are withdrawn from them. But the other key, which is called the key of jurisdiction, is communicated also to other ministers of the Church, who are not priests.

AXIOM LI.

Wherein the Keys are to be exercised.

Although the force and efficacy of the keys, in itself, embraces all things, yet, by reason of defect of jurisdiction, a priest of the New Law cannot, except in time of necessity, exercise the power of the keys on that which is not subjected to him, nor yet promiscuously on all those which are subjected to him; for there are certain crimes, the examination and absolution of which the priests of higher dignity have reserved to themselves. Nevertheless, a superior priest may extend to an inferior the jurisdiction and power of absolving him.

AXIOM LII.

The Definition and Force of Excommunication.

The doctors rightly deliver that Excommunication is a separation from the communion of the Church, from reception of fruit therefrom, and participation in the general suffrages thereof. And, albeit, this kind of punishment be most grievous, yet it is laudably employed by the Catholick Church, following the example of God Himself, in order to break down the contumacy of wicked and rebellious men, even if in external goods only they have injured others; and such force has it that even an unjustly inflicted excommunication very frequently has power and attains its effects, namely—when the error committed is not such as to take away the authority of the sentence.

AXIOM LIII.

Who may Excommunicate and be Excommunicated.

Since, in order to carry out a sentence of excommunication, there must needs be authority of jurisdiction, *in foro exteriori*, neither excommunicated nor suspended priests, to whom the use of that jurisdiction has been interdicted; and not all priests, and not priests alone, but those only whose province it is, according to the laws of ecclesiastical discipline, be they or be they not priests, may exercise this function. Since jurisdiction has regard to inferiors, one may excommunicate neither himself, nor his equal, nor his superior. The Church forbids the condemnation of a whole multitude of people to the pain of anathema, lest perchance the innocent be involved in like condemnation with the guilty. He who has been once cast out from the company of the faithful may be a second and third time excommunicated.

AXIOM LIV.

The Fellowship of the Excommunicated to be Avoided.

Familiarity and intercourse with one lying under the *lesser* excommunication is not forbidden, but he who associates with one lying under the greater excommunication, even in matters pertaining to the body, unless spiritual benefit, obligation, or necessity hold him excused, sins grievously; and without doubt does so, if by consulting, aiding, or otherwise abetting, he be made partaker of the crime of him who has been excommunicated, or enter into association with him in Divine things, or otherwise to the contempt of the Church: he sins venially if he have the same intercourse in any other way. The punishment of those who violate this prohibition is variously ordained: for if the sentence of excommunication embrace also those having intercourse with the excommunicated, or if any one, by consulting, aiding, or otherwise, be made partaker of the crime, then, without doubt, he who associates with the excommunicated, the cases mentioned being excepted, incurs the greater excommunication, others only the lesser excommunication.

AXIOM LV.

The Absolution of the Excommunicated.

Any priest soever may absolve those who are placed under him from the penalty of the lesser excommunication, and from that of the greater likewise, if it have been inflicted by law, six cases only excepted, which are copiously explained by S. Thomas. But if the greater excommunication be inflicted by a judge, *extra mortis necessitatem*, the judge who inflicted it only, or his superior prelate, has power to remove it, which power he can use even against the will of him who is bound by the anathema. This likewise is certain—that if any one be condemned by more than one excommunication, although sometimes all may be taken away together, yet one being taken away the rest remain, especially if they have been inflicted by different judges.

AXIOM LVI.

The Power of Indulgences.

Seeing Indulgences may be produced from the infinite treasury of the Church, they may doubtless be lawfully granted, on the concurrence of three things, viz., of authority on the part of the granter, of charity on the part of the recipient, and of piety on the part of their cause, and they avail so far as their terms indicate. Wherefore, it is not to be doubted that they have power of remitting by way of satisfaction punishment, those punishments even which have to be endured in purgatory: they may laudably be granted in order to spiritual benefit in return for a temporal subsidy.

AXIOM LVII.

The Granting of Indulgences.

Plenary power of granting Indulgences resides in the supreme Pontiff, the lawful successor of S. Peter: an ordinary power in the Bishops, limited by his appointment: and a committed power in Legates, be they or be they not priests. But in all these, be they saints or sinners, the power remains of one and the same efficacy.

AXIOM LVIII.

Whom do Indulgences Profit?

Those still in the bonds of mortal sin are in no way capable of receiving the grace of indulgences, but those who have their souls free therefrom, monks as well as men in any other state of life, not excepting the granters of the indulgences themselves, may obtain the grace, by observing the conditions described in the letters of indulgence.

AXIOM LIX.

Solemn Penance.

For many very grave causes, in order to expiate certain crimes, those especially whereby a whole communion is excited, public and solemn penance is laudably enjoined on laics, as well women as men; and seeing it contains a signification of the expulsion of Adam from Paradise, and a profession of perpetual sorrow for sin, it would be contrary to its nature to be repeated, or decreed to be oftener than once undergone by the same persons.

OF THE SACRAMENT OF EXTREME UNCTION.

AXIOM LX.

Its Institution, Matter, and Form.

Extreme Unction is a Sacrament, single in number, promulgated indeed by the Apostles, but first instituted by Christ. Its fitting and appropriate matter is olive oil, consecrated by a Bishop, this deprecation being its legitimate form:—By this holy anointing, and by His most piteous mercy, the Lord pardon thee whereinsoever thou hast done amiss by seeing; by this holy anointing, and by His most piteous mercy, the Lord pardon thee whereinsoever thou hast done amiss by hearing; by this holy anointing, and by His most piteous mercy, the Lord pardon thee whereinsoever thou hast done amiss by smelling; by this holy anointing, and by His most piteous mercy, the Lord pardon thee whereinsoever thou hast done amiss by tasting and speaking; by this holy anointing, and by His most piteous mercy, the Lord pardon thee whereinsoever thou hast done amiss by touching; by this holy anointing, and by His most piteous mercy, the Lord pardon thee whereinsoever thou hast done amiss by walking.

AXIOM LXI.

Its Effect.

The Sacrament of Extreme Unction does not imprint *character*, but avails, in the first place and principally, to the curing of the imbecility of the soul, contracted from deadly sin, and the restoring it to health and strength, along with the destruction of sin, if sin there be found in the soul. It avails, in the second place, to the healing of bodily disease. It does not always, however, produce this effect; then only when it is expedient for the salvation of the recipient, and when he opposes to it no impediment.

AXIOM LXII.

Its Minister.

The administration of Extreme Unction does not pertain to the condition of a deacon, much less to that of a laic, but to the office of a priest alone, be he or be he not a bishop.

AXIOM LXIII.

On whom it is to be conferred; and to what parts of the body its matter is to be applied.

The Sacrament of Extreme Unction is to be administered to men of mature age and not to children, to persons of sane mind and not to madmen, to those in peril of death and not to those who are but slightly indisposed. Its matter is to be applied, not to the whole body, but to these six parts—the eyes, the ears, the nostrils, the mouth, the hands, and the feet; to which parts may be added also the reins. If it so happen that the sick person is deprived of any of these parts, the part nearest to the part lacking is to be anointed in its place.

AXIOM LXIV.

Iteration.

Since Extreme Unction is not of the number of those sacraments whose effect is perpetual, it may, without injury to its dignity, be iterated, not only in diverse diseases, but even during the progress of the same disease, if it be of long continuance, as in the case of consumption or dropsy.

OF THE SACRAMENT OF ORDER.

AXIOM LXV.

(Partly from S. Thomas, partly from the Decree of Eugenius the Fourth delivered to the Armenians.)

Its Definition and Parts.

Order is a Sacrament of the Church, and necessary, whereby by outward signs, inward and spiritual power is granted to the ordained. The matter of this Sacrament is that by the delivery of which the order is conferred, as the priesthood is conferred by the delivery of a chalice with wine, and a paten with bread; the diaconate by the delivery of a Book of the Gospels; the subdiaconate by the delivery of an empty chalice with an empty paten placed upon it; and similarly the other orders by a signification of the things pertaining to their several ministries. The form of the priesthood is: Receive power to offer sacrifice in the Church for the living and for the dead, in the name of the Father, and of the Son, and of the Holy Ghost. If any one wish to see the forms of the other orders, here omitted for brevity's sake, he will find them set forth at length in the Roman Pontifical.

AXIOM LXVI.

Its Effects.

In the conferring of every order there is given grace *gratum faciens*, and there is imprinted *character* which requires, in order to its reception, the previous character of baptism, of necessity—of confirmation, of congruity—and of the lower order, of ecclesiastical constitution.

AXIOM LXVII.

The Quality of its Receiver.

Although he who promotes an unworthy person to any of the sacred orders, and he who, with a consciousness of deadly sin, receives, or having received, uses any sacred order, do alike most grievously sin; yet goodness of life is not necessary to the reception of order *ex parte* of the Sacrament, but only *ex parte* of the Divine precept. Similarly also, knowledge of the Scripture is required in him who receives order—not absolute knowledge, but knowledge sufficient for the right performance of the functions pertaining to that order. But albeit virtue and knowledge do exceedingly become those who are to be or have been ordained, yet of themselves they can confer order on no man.

AXIOM LXVIII.

The Distinction of Orders.

According to the number of the ministries, necessary for the consecration and reverent treatment of the Eucharist, seven orders of clerks have been instituted. And of these the three highest, as occupied about the consecrated matter, are rightly named sacred; the others, as occupied about the matter not yet consecrated, are not called sacred. Those orders are distinguished one from another, which have each special and definite functions. It belongs to an *ostiarius* to guard the door of the temple, to admit the worthy, to debar the unworthy: to a reader to recite the lessons, and declare to the people the oracles of the prophets: to an exorcist, by exorcisms to deliver energumens and catechumens from the vexations of demons: to an acolyte to prepare the lights in the sacrarium, to carry a wax taper, and to serve the sub-deacon with the cruets of wine and water: to a sub-deacon to serve the bishop, priest, and deacon with basin, water, and towel, for the washing of their hands, to read the epistle, to receive their offerings from the people, and to place them on the altar, or deliver them to the deacon, also to give to the deacon the paten and chalice, and to pour into the chalice wine and water: to a deacon to assist the priest, and to minister to him, especially in the sacraments of Baptism, Confirmation, and the Eucharist, to arrange the Lord's Table, to bear the Cross, to explain to the people the Epistle and Gospel, and to dispense to them the Blood of the Lord: to priests to absolve, to bind, to bless God's gifts, and principally to consecrate the Sacrament of the Lord's Body and Blood. The priest receives his sacerdotal *character* when there is delivered to him a chalice with a certain form of words.

AXIOM LXIX.

The Minister of Order.

Only a bishop can confer the Sacrament of Order, and this power of his neither suspension nor heresy have any force to take away, provided he use the proper form with due intention. But he who is ordained by a suspended or heretical bishop, does not, by reason of the obstacle of sin which is in him, thereby receive grace, nor can he use the order he has received, by reason of the defect of jurisdiction in him who ordained him.

AXIOM LXX.

Impediments to Order.

Children as yet without the use of reason, slaves who are under the dominion of others, homicides who have polluted their hands with human blood, bastards, and those who are in any way notably deformed or mutilated, are debarred, not of sacramental necessity, but of ecclesiastical precept, from the reception of sacred orders. Women are debarred of sacramental necessity. They would in no way receive order, even were it outwardly conferred on them. The others would indeed receive it, albeit it was done wickedly, and contrary to the constitution of the Church.

AXIOM LXXI.

Certain matters connected with Order.

Tonsure is not an order, nor does it deprive one of the power of holding earthly possessions, yet clerks of every order ought to wear it, as containing a signification of a spiritual kingship, and a more excellent perfection, and of a withdrawal of the mind from fleeting things to things divine and sempiternal. Similarly the episcopal dignity is not to be reckoned in the number of the sacred orders. It is, nevertheless, necessary to the Church in order to the preparation of the people for rightly receiving the Eucharist, as is also the authority of the Supreme Pontiff, which is superior to the episcopate, to secure the unity of Christians and the binding of them together into one body. If any man marvel at the variety of vestments used by the ministers of the Church, let him know that some offices are common to all the ministers of the Church, while others are peculiarly appropriate to certain orders, and to signify that, certain vestments are common to all orders, certain others special to each.

The Sacrament of Matrimony.

AXIOM LXXII.

Matrimony as an Office of Nature.

Although Matrimony be of the natural law, and the matrimonial act be not only lawful, but frequently also laudable and worthy of reward, as when, for instance, it is performed either in payment of the marriage debt, or to generate offspring for the worship of God, yet no man is in these days obliged to contract matrimony by necessity of any precept.

AXIOM LXXIII.

Matrimony as a Sacrament.

Matrimony, by reason of divers things which concur in it, has been instituted at divers times. For, if you regard procreation of children, it had its origin in the estate of innocence: if a remedy for the wound of sin—in the period between the fall of Adam and the law of Moses: if the defining of certain persons who are fit for it—in the old law: if the mystery of the union of Christ with His Church—in the new law: if the friendship and mutual service of the spouses—in the civil law. According to all these institutions—the first and last excepted—Matrimony is rightly called a sacrament. According to that institution which it received in the time of the Gospel, it is a sacrament of the new law, conferring grace in order to the right performance of those things which concern it. The second perfection of this, as of all other kinds of Matrimony, and which consists in operation, requires sexual connection, but not its first perfection, which consists in the powers given in order to this operation.

AXIOM LXXIV.

Espousals.

Espousals are none else than a promise of future nuptials. Those are capable of contracting espousals who have attained to or have passed the seventh year of their age. They are dissolved for various causes: by law, for two causes, viz., intervening matrimony, effected by words *de præsenti*, with another, and profession of the religious life: by judgment of the Church, for many other reasons, which it would take too long to enumerate.

AXIOM LXXV.

Definition of Matrimony.

Matrimony is rightly defined by the Master to be the marital conjunction of a man and a woman, being legitimate persons, who retain an undivided manner of life. It has obtained a name appropriate to its effect, for a woman marries for this that she may sometime become a mother (*mater fiat*). It is called also wedlock and nuptials; wedlock from its nature: nuptials from its efficient cause.

AXIOM LXXVI.

Matrimonial Consent.

Mutual consent between man and woman, expressed openly or secretly, in words designating *present* time, is the true efficient cause of matrimony.

AXIOM LXXVII.

Matrimonial Consent confirmed by oath or carnal connection.

An oath added to consent declared by words designating *future* time, does not effect matrimony. But carnal connection, if it follow such consent, will, unless there be evident appearance of fraud, cause the matrimony to be ratified and confirmed *in foro* of the Church, albeit, *in foro* of one's conscience, there can arise no matrimony without a true assent of the will.

AXIOM LXXVIII.

Matrimonial Consent compelled; and conditionally expressed.

Consent extorted by fear falling on a "constant" man, destroys matrimony, *ex parte* as well of the compeller as of the compelled. Nay, nor can a father, by his authority, compel his son to take a wife. Consent suspended by a condition imposed, sometimes effects, and sometimes does not effect matrimony. For if the condition imposed have respect to the present time, whether it be honourable or base, matters not, so that it be not repugnant to the goods of matrimony; similarly, if the condition be necessary, whatever time it have respect to, the consent has force to effect matrimony.

But if the condition be in the genus of things fortuitous, and refer to future time, consent expressed subject to such a condition does not suffice to effect matrimony, any more than if it were expressed in words of future time.

AXIOM LXXIX.

The Object of Matrimonial Consent.

Matrimonial consent, whose proper and prime object is not sexual connection, but social union, properly and *per se* has regard to the generation of offspring, and the avoidance of fornication. The spouses, in contracting matrimony, may propose to themselves other ends, honourable or base, but these are fortuitously and improperly called ends, and do not redound to the goodness or badness of the wedlock.

AXIOM LXXX.

The Goods of Matrimony.

Of the three goods of matrimony, to wit, fidelity, offspring, and sacramentality, whereby is excused the matrimony and its acts, sacramentality holds the first place These goods of matrimony, at least offspring and fidelity, under which is comprehended due payment of the marriage debt, are so necessary in order to the honourableness of the matrimonial act, that those who have intercourse with their wives solely to satisfy their lusts and appetites do always sin—mortally if the ardour of lust lead them beyond the bounds of matrimony; venially if it be contained within them.

AXIOM LXXXI.

Impediments of Matrimony in genere.

The prohibition of the Church, and that time which is commonly called ferial, hinders the contracting of matrimony, but the things contained in the following versicles destroy the contract, viz.:—

        Error, conditio, votum, cognatio, crimen
        Cultus disparitas, vis, ordo, ligamen, honestas,
        Si sis affinis, si fortè coire nequibis.

AXIOM LXXXII.

The Impediment of Error.

Error committed as to condition, as well as to person, naturally impedes matrimony.

AXIOM LXXXIII.

The Impediment of Servitude.

Although in order that a slave may take a wife, his lord's consent is not necessary, yet ignorance of his estate of slavery renders his matrimonial contract null and void, his slavery preventing the due payment of the marriage debt. Nevertheless, he who, while a freeman, has contracted matrimony, may, before dissolution of the marriage, and even against the will of his wife, surrender himself in bondage to another. The civil laws, to which the laws ecclesiastical assent, ordain as to the offspring of parents of different conditions, that in those things which pertain to personal condition they follow the mother, while in those things which pertain to dignity they follow the father.

AXIOM LXXXIV.

The Impediments of Vow and Order.

A solemn, but not a simple, vow has force to destroy the contract of matrimony. Although from matrimony, even while it yet endures, an entrance is permitted to the sacred orders: yet from the sacred orders, by reason of the vow of continence annexed to them, a man may in no way turn back to matrimony.

AXIOM LXXXV.

The Impediment of Consanguinity.

Propinquity of blood, or, as it is commonly called, consanguinity, is none other than a bond between those who descend from the same root or principle, contracted by corporal propagation, and distinguished by certain degrees and lines, which destroys the matrimony extrinsically celebrated, by the natural law, between a parent and his offspring; by the old law between those persons to one of whom pertained the guardianship of the other's chastity: and by ecclesiastical constitution, between those between whom there is a conjunction and communion of blood by a transverse line within the fifth degree.

AXIOM LXXXVI.

The Impediment of Affinity.

Affinity is a kind of propinquity contracted from marriage, from illicit connection, from espousals, but not from another affinity, and remains even unto death between the persons whom it has once united. It impedes and destroys matrimony in the same way as propinquity of blood, and from propinquity of blood its degrees, their distinction and extension, are taken. To destroy the matrimony the process must be by way of accusation and production of witnesses.

AXIOM LXXXVII.

The Impediment of Spiritual Cognation.

Of spiritual cognation, which springs partly from the Sacrament of Baptism, and partly from that of Confirmation, there are three species, commonly known among ecclesiastical writers by the names of spiritual paternity, compaternity, and spiritual fraternity. Spiritual paternity exists between the god-parent and the baptized or confirmed, also between the baptizer or confirmer and the baptized or confirmed; compaternity, between the god-parent, the baptizer or confirmer, and the parents of the baptized or confirmed; and spiritual fraternity between the baptized or confirmed and the natural offspring of their god-parent. All these species of cognation cross over from the husband to the wife, and *e diverso* from the wife to the husband. If they arise previous to, but not if subsequent to the consummation of the matrimony, they not only hinder contracting it, but destroy it if contracted. But if either of the spouses, without any compelling necessity, contract such spiritual cognation, it deprives him or her of the right of *exacting* the marriage debt.

AXIOM LXXXVIII.

The Impediment of Civil Cognation.

Adoption is the election of an extraneous person into the place of a son or daughter, nephew or niece. Hence arises a civil cognation, which is threefold—first, between the adopter and the adopted and his offspring ; second, between the adopted and the natural son or daughter of the adopter ; and third, between the wife of the adopter and the adopted, or between the wife of the adopted, and the father adopting. Of these, the first and third always, and the second, so long as the adopted is under the power of him by whom he has been adopted, impede matrimony.

AXIOM LXXXIX.

The Impediments of Natural Frigidity, Malformation, Insanity, Incest, and Immature Age.

Both by reason of natural frigidity, not arising from defect of age, and by reason of perpetual impotence arising from malformation, proved by a three years' experiment, the spouses are separated by authority of the Church. In the separation by reason of impotence arising from malformation, to both of the spouses, but in the other case to the woman only, is permitted a free power of entering into a fresh wedlock ; but so, nevertheless, that if at any time the faculty of connection be restored to the first husband, the woman leaving her second must return to her former husband. Perpetual insanity, and insanity which at the time of entering on the matrimony deprived the mind of the use of reason, impedes matrimony, and destroys it if contracted. Similarly, incest with the sister of one's future wife, committed either before espousals or in the interval between the espousals and the matrimony ; but if committed subsequent to the marriage it does not destroy it, but deprives him by whom it has been committed of his right of demanding payment of the marriage debt. He is interdicted, moreover, by the Church, on the death of his wife, from taking another. Immature age, moreover, is an impediment, reckoned in the male beneath his fourteenth, in the female beneath her twelfth year, unless vigour of judgment compensate what is lacking in years.

AXIOM XC.

The Impediment of Disparity of Religion.

Although a believer cannot contract valid and lawful matrimony with an unbeliever, nevertheless, that is true matrimony which unbelievers celebrate among themselves ; yet, however, if one of the spouses embrace the faith while the other persists in error, the one who has embraced the faith is not bound either to pay the marriage debt or to cohabit with the other, although at the same time he retains the power of doing both. And what is more, if the perversity of him who remains an unbeliever proceed even to an obstinate contumely of his Creator, the believing spouse—the previous marriage being dissolved—has the power of entering on a fresh union, which power would not be granted for any infidelity or other crime whatsoever.

AXIOM XCI.

Uxoricide.

The civil laws permit the aggrieved husband, on his own authority, to slay his wife taken in the act of adultery. But the ecclesiastical laws ordain that in the punishment of this as of other crimes, publick authority must be waited for, and the matter proceeded with according to the zeal of justice, and not of vengeance and hatred. They entirely condemn the slaughter of a wife on one's own authority, and number it among capital crimes. They therefore decree that matrimony, to be contracted in respect of any woman soever, is thereby impeded; and contracted with a paramour, in the hope of marrying whom the crime was perpetrated, is thereby destroyed.

AXIOM XCII.

Dissolution of Matrimony by Solemn Vow.

In like manner as the corporal bond of matrimony is loosed by corporal death, so the spiritual bond of matrimony which exists between the spouses, while their matrimony is not yet consummated, is loosed by a solemn profession of the monastick life, which is a kind of spiritual death. Hence, to either of the spouses before union of their bodies, is granted a free power of entering on the religious life, and to the other who is left in the world of marrying whom he will. But after consummation of their matrimony, to neither of the spouses is it lawful to enter on the religious or monastick estate of life, or on new nuptials during the lifetime of the other.

AXIOM XCIII.

Divorce for Fornication, in time of the Gospel.

To a husband it is always lawful, so far as regards his bed, on his own authority, and as regards cohabitation, by authority of the Church, to put away a fornicating wife, with the exception of a few cases. But this, albeit allowed, is not commanded, unless indeed the wife be obstinately determined to continue in her shame. The same rights pertain to a wife in regard to her adulterous husband. Their divorce having been accomplished, each of the spouses is, during the lifetime of the other, precluded from entering on new nuptials—but not from a mutual reconciliation, provided there be in him, who by his guilt has merited his repudiation, an amendment of his former life.

AXIOM XCIV.

Second Nuptials.

The most approved doctors of Catholick truth hold that second, third, and subsequent marriages are lawful, inasmuch as the bond of the former marriage is broken by the death of the other spouse; and that they, no less than the first marriage, have sacramental dignity, inasmuch as there may be discerned in them both the matter and form of lawful matrimony.

AXIOM XCV.

Matrimonialis debiti persolutio.

Non modo apertè poscenti, sed etiam aliquo signo indicanti, debet uterque conjugum, ex æquo, incolumitate et honestate salvâ, alteri, etiam tempore sacro, licet tunc petens levitèr saltem peccet, matrimoniale debitum persolvere; ob idque neuter eorum sine alterius consensû, talis continentiæ voto, quo istius debiti persolutio impediretur, se obstringere potest.

AXIOM XCVI.

Polygamy.

Although a multitude of wives be repugnant to the secondary end of matrimony, and is so in some measure a turning aside from the natural law, yet in the first ages, it was by Divine dispensation permitted to certain men to have many wives. But to have a concubine, with whom no right of matrimony exists, and which is prejudicial to the primary end of matrimony, to wit, the education of offspring, is violently opposed to the natural law, and was never allowed at any time, but the Church of God hath always judged a society of persons so congregated to be impious, and their intercourse abominable and to be numbered among deadly sins.

AXIOM XCVII.

Irregularity.

A second marriage, either according to or against the law, entered into either before or after baptism, as well as a first marriage contracted with a woman who was not a virgin, debars a man from the sacred orders of clerks, or, to use a trite word, causes an irregularity, which, however, being of human law, may be taken away by dispensation of the Supreme Pontiff in respect of all the orders, and in respect of the inferior or minor orders, by dispensation of other bishops.

AXIOM XCVIII.

The Writ of Repudiation in time of the Law.

Although matrimony be, by nature, indissoluble, nevertheless its dissolution falls under the Divine dispensation. Hence the opinion of those is probable, although it is the less common one, who assert that during the period of the law of Moses, it was, by Divine concession, lawful for a man to repudiate his wife, and for the woman so repudiated to marry another husband, but not to return to her former husband, for that the law expressly forbade. In the Writ of Repudiation which was given to the wife, its causes, among which the proximate cause was hatred of her, were not to be written severally and specially, but generally only.

AXIOM XCIX.

Illegitimate Offspring.

Those who are born of temporary unions, and out of true wedlock, are called illegitimate, and both civil and ecclesiastical laws debar them from hereditary succession to the paternal goods, and from certain functions and dignities; at the same time they point out and open to them manifold ways of arriving at the dignity and condition of lawful children.

Ad majorem Dei gloriam.

www.ingramcontent.com/pod-product-compliance
Lightning Source LLC
Chambersburg PA
CBHW032132160426
43197CB00008B/611